RISKY GOSPEL

ABANDON FEAR *and* BUILD
SOMETHING AWESOME

OWEN STRACHAN

NELSON
BOOKS

An Imprint of Thomas Nelson

To R. Albert Mohler Jr., whose teaching and courageous example have encouraged a generation of Christians to live boldly for Christ

Published in Nashville, Tennessee, by Nelson Books, an imprint of Thomas Nelson. Nelson Books and Thomas Nelson are registered trademarks of HarperCollins Christian Publishing, Inc.

Published in association with the literary agency of Wolgemuth & Associates, Inc.

Thomas Nelson, Inc., titles may be purchased in bulk for educational, business, fund-raising, or sales promotional use. For information, please e-mail SpecialMarkets@ThomasNelson.com.

Unless otherwise indicated, Scripture quotations are taken from THE ENGLISH STANDARD VERSION. © 2001 by Crossway Bibles, a division of Good News Publishers.

Scripture quotations marked KJV are taken from the Holy Bible, King James Version (public domain).

Scripture quotations marked MSG are taken from *The Message* by Eugene H. Peterson. © 1993, 1994, 1995, 1996, 2000. Used by permission of NavPress Publishing Group. All rights reserved.

Scripture quotations marked NASB are taken from the NEW AMERICAN STANDARD BIBLE®, © The Lockman Foundation 1960, 1962, 1963, 1968, 1971, 1972, 1973, 1975, 1977, 1995. Used by permission.

Scripture quotations marked NKJV are taken from the NEW KING JAMES VERSION. © 1982 by Thomas Nelson, Inc. Used by permission. All rights reserved.

Library of Congress Cataloging-in-Publication Data

Strachan, Owen.
  Risky gospel : abandon fear and build something awesome / Owen Strachan.
    pages cm
  ISBN 978-1-4002-0579-0
1. Spiritual formation. 2. Christian life. I. Title.
  BV4511.S76 2013
  248.4--dc23

2013017252

Printed in the United States of America

13 14 15 16 17 18 RRD 6 5 4 3 2 1

CONTENTS

FOREWORD

by Kyle Idleman, author of Not a Fan *and* Gods at War

WHEN WAS THE LAST TIME YOU DID SOMETHING THAT was a little bit risky? I don't mean "use the bathrooms at the local fast-food taco place" risky, I mean something truly risky. Rapid heartbeat, sweaty palms, shortness of breath—that kind of risky. When was the last time you did something that was both exhilarating and terrifying all at the same time?

The combined tonic of excitement and terror seems to be a favorite of my brothers-in-law. They are always building a too-tall deer stand or preparing to hunt down wild boar and wrestle them unarmed. If you ask one of my brothers-in-law about his hobbies he'll tell you about rappelling out of helicopters and lighting marijuana fields on fire. Occasionally when I am with them, they'll be getting ready to go out on one of these adventures and they'll look at me with farmland fire in their eyes and say, "Kyle, you gotta come with us!"

I typically pass on those kinds of outings. My in-laws may be deer hunters and boar wrestlers, but me? Not so much. I'm not what you would call a risk chaser. I'm a book reader. I'm a web surfer. I'm a sushi eater. I don't take risks with wild animals. It goes against my nature, my character, my life experience. See, I didn't grow up on a farm, I don't own a pair of cowboy boots, and the only pet I had growing up was a goldfish (an especially tame goldfish, I might add).

We use the word *risky* to define something that doesn't just diverge from making sense but can, in fact, go in the opposite direction of good sense. In my mind it seems risky for anyone to chase after a wild animal. But for me especially, this goes in the opposite direction of my comfort level, of who I am and what I've learned over the years.

Many of you have similar notions—maybe it's not about hunting animals, but we've all learned to navigate risks. In the Gospels, however, I've found a Jesus who doesn't shy away from risk. I've found a Jesus that calls me to abandon all the things I thought would bring me safety. I've found a Jesus who takes the world's common sense about risk management and asks his followers to live in ways that seem dangerously counterintuitive.

Risky Gospel is a road map for the Christian who wants to move from spiritual risk manager to fearless follower, and you couldn't ask for a more gutsy guide than Owen Strachan. I believe Owen has been emboldened by God to reveal the kind of arrested spiritual development so many of us have witnessed and experienced.

Owen takes the modern Christ follower's life from mere principle—where so many of us are content to remain—to urgently practical, which is in itself inherently risky. In these pages, I could sense an author who was willing to live out the risks to which he's calling readers. I believe the practical steps laid out in each of these chapters will be of benefit to Christians who need to take some healthy, God-glorifying risks.

Owen's insights are piercing and the stories he mines from his own life, from today's world, and from history are worthwhile narratives that deserve to be told and imprinted on our hearts. Better still, Owen's ability to charm and disarm had me laughing at *Office* quotes one moment and questioning my innermost motives the next. But in a world of quotable tweets and YouTube attention spans, Owen has a knack for keeping us interested for more than 140 characters.

I'll finish with a brief confession. I have, on occasion, been dragged out into the woods to hunt with my in-laws. In the speckled shade of trees, waiting in the quiet for heaven only knows what beast, I've felt the rapid heartbeat, the sweaty palms, the shortness of breath. These are the moments when we've chosen something risky. I've seen the same feeling wash over those making spiritual commitments at our weekend church services. To those folks, coming down to talk to a pastor was risky—maybe even more risky than hunting wild animals. But in those risky moments, lives change. But the truth is, no matter where you are in your spiritual journey, whether you are taking first steps or are a lifelong believer, the call to living out the risky gospel is for you.

Prepare your heart for rapid beats. Prepare your palms for condensation. Prepare your lungs for short breaths. Join Owen in rediscovering a gospel that compels us to risk our lives for Jesus Christ.

1 WEAK CHRISTIANS: YOUR STRESSED LIFE NOW

The average man doesn't want to be free. He wants to be safe.

—H. L. MENCKEN, *The American Mercury*

MANY YEARS AGO, IN A STATE FAR, FAR AWAY, A SIXTEEN-year-old boy crouched, trying to seize the courage necessary to jump off a rock into the waiting water below. In front of several friends and (even worse) a number of total strangers, he waited in place, searching furiously for the courage to (a) move forward and (b) jump into the water so as not to forever embarrass himself and future generations of his lineage.

Quivering, legs trembling, face strained, he waited, summoning boldness to come forth like a wizard daring a dragon to strike. It was a rite of passage in coastal Maine. A bunch of young guys find a rock, goad one another on, and jump into the water, thereby proving at some deep psychological level their manhood. Like so many challenges of this kind, it was almost profound in its simplicity: We go find big rock. We jump off. We pound chests afterward.

It did not happen. The royal *we*—specifically *I*—could not do it.

What happened in this moment? My mother, no doubt learning of this event for the first time in these very pages, would commend me for my decision. She might say that I exercised wisdom. She would likely be right.

What happened was a failure of boldness. There was, I suppose, a minimal amount of what insurance agents might call "mitigating circumstances" present. It was *possible* that something could go wrong. In reality, though, the odds of success were quite high. I could see where I wanted to go; I had the power to get there; but I simply could not make it happen. It wasn't a failure of physicality that stopped me. It was a failure of *will*. There was an element of risk involved, and that element stopped me in my tracks.

I've thought about this moment often since it occurred. I don't regret it, exactly, and I have little interest in spurring on a culture of cliff-diving. In fact, I'm not sure that true manhood necessarily overlaps with such feats, however impressive they may be. But there was a parable in that moment that has repeatedly come to mind since that day. The takeaway was this: There are going to be moments in life, perhaps many, when it is not your circumstances that paralyze you. It is not physical or mental inability. It is not lack of capacity. No, what will stop you dead in your tracks is more simple.

It will be a lack of boldness. It will be a failure to see the power of God, and to risk everything in this world to gain him.

Jumping off a rock is not a big deal. But there really will be important moments, far more consequential times in life, when all of us will find ourselves seemingly unable to move. We will see where we need to go; we will be aware that nothing really has to stop us from getting there; and yet we will still stand, legs or heart aquiver, and not go forward. We want to grow in our faith and get into the Bible on a daily basis, but we can't quite muster up the spiritual energy. We realize that we need a bigger plan for our families and careers, and we want to develop it, but we're afraid to actually define our situation.

Better to stay in a neutral zone, keep expectations low, and not have to do anything drastic. That's what we're really afraid of: drastic, life-upsetting action.

So we play it safe, keep things calm . . . and stay stuck.

I wonder if this isn't an increasingly common situation today for many Christians. It's not that we *want* to be where we are. It's not that we are trying to stand still. We see a good goal and want to move toward it. But something, some kind of invisible force field, holds us back.

If you have felt this—if you feel this—then you are in good company. Maybe you didn't expect to be here, thinking these thoughts. Maybe you thought the Christian life, and life in a country seemingly friendly to biblical faith, was going to be a smoother ride than this. Let's walk through how you may have found yourself thinking this, and what might be influencing you and me to struggle to be bold.

YOUR STRESSED LIFE NOW

The Christian life, according to some of our most prominent teachers and leaders, is like a journey into space that never ends. You make your way through it with the same slightly stunned smile that you have after a long and pleasant nap. You're looking at the world, and everything is dreamy and vaguely sleepy and relaxing. You find that life magically trends upward.

Life is one long exercise in uninterrupted fulfillment.

What does this mean practically? It means that finances climb, marriages naturally mature, kids pop out of bed in the mornings like cheerful groundhogs, the coffee is always at just the right temperature, work yields promotions you didn't expect, the rain avoids you when you're running outdoors, and through it all you smile a dreamy smile, living in a state of cheerful surprise.

It's like a cereal commercial, all health and good cheer, except it never stops. God is the one who activates all this. If you're not experiencing such a life, goes the thinking, you can know that you're destined to. It's just around the corner. There's something wrong with your faith, maybe; you're not trusting enough, or you haven't had a crisis experience, and if you'll just surrender it all (and, by the way, buy the book and DVDs of a major guru), you'll get there, and all your difficulties will just *evaporate*.

But you know what intrudes? Reality. Life can actually be pretty tough, even if you are blessed to know the Lord. Not everyone is nice. Sometimes things are really difficult, and the clouds don't easily lift. There's a freedom in saying that out loud, isn't there? Ironic, I think, but true. As the old Scot said, confession is good for the soul.[1] Why? Because, much as it can be hard to admit it, life in any age is challenging. This is true of our day and age. We *are* living in uncertain times. Smash-you-up times. Grind-you-down times.

And we don't always know where we're going, or even how to begin.

How about this? Let's look for a few pages at what daily

existence *really* can be like. Then we'll get to some encouraging material that will provide truly inspiring uplift.

THESE ARE THE TIMES THAT TRY OUR SOULS

We are living in troubled times. The economy crashed in 2008, the worst such crisis in eighty years. Things have gotten better in some ways, but we're still not through it. We've seen a good many ups and not a few downs in the broader world. Meanwhile, many of us know people who are still out of work—or who are patching work together just to make ends meet. Newspapers pump out articles that tell the story of swaths of the population that have yet to get back on their feet—consultants who no longer have a field, municipal employees whose jobs disappeared overnight from small towns, graphic designers who can't string enough freelance jobs together, near retirees whose savings have been halved.

Perhaps this crisis is not merely "out there," felt in houses of commerce and businesses of scale. Perhaps it's directly affected you. These are uncertain times for many of us—and uncertainty easily breeds fear and worry.

Or maybe you're feeling the toughness of life in other respects. You want to be a Christian, but it seems as if the pressure is ratcheting up on you. You've always believed that marriage means the union of a man and a woman who become a husband and a wife. This kind of conviction wasn't formerly a position of bigotry—it was common sense. But recently, your coworkers—generally likable and helpful—got heated when the subject of gay marriage came up. They called those who champion biblical marriage "backward" and "hateful." Your face red, you haltingly mentioned you know some Christians, and they're pretty nice people.

Nobody shouted at you, but their chilled silence showed you what they thought of your opinions.

Later, you logged on to Facebook to seek out some support, but you found your old college classmates—the ones you roomed with for two years and shared every facet of life with—attacking a blog post that said homosexuality was wrong. You've seen anger before, but nothing like this. It was rage heated to a flame. It scared you.

You expected this persecution for some major leader, Billy Graham and similar types, but that's not you. You're just a nice person who's never had an enemy in her life.

Why has the world gotten so hostile so fast toward Christians?

DUDE, WHERE'S MY ROAD MAP?

Or it could be that you feel as though there's no road map anymore. Sure, there's always Google Maps or your iPhone for a road trip. But when it comes to a life plan, such guidance doesn't really exist. A lot of twentysomethings sense that something is missing, that they don't have a key life ingredient that their grandparents did. Everything seemed so clear and obvious for them, at least when they told you about their early lives. They went to college (or didn't), got a job, got married, dedicated themselves to their calling for about six decades, then retired. Along the way, kids came along, white picket fences were constructed, and life's challenges were hurdled.

It may feel as if everyone else, in fact, *has* embarked on that kind of life, but you're stuck. College debt is coming out your ears. You're making $22,000 a year before taxes. The opposite sex at your church doesn't seem to know you exist, despite the impressive efforts of the college-and-career pastor. (Art night! Baseball outing! Theater-and-dinner!) You moved to a thriving city to jump-start your career and make good on that absolutely necessary, can't-miss, $150,000 education, and yet you realize that the urban loft may have evaporated into thin air, to be replaced by the luxury suite known as your parents' basement bedroom, half-finished and sawdusty.

The news media are flush with these kinds of stories. Here's a section from one about "Generation Limbo":

> When Stephanie Kelly, a 2009 graduate of the University of Florida, looked for a job in her chosen field, advertising, she found few prospects and even fewer takers. So now she has two jobs: as a part-time "senior secretary" at the Florida Museum of Natural History in Gainesville and a freelance gig writing for Elfster.com, a "secret Santa" Web site.[2]

If this kind of coverage applies to you, you may be aware that, on the whole, you're not old. Middle age is a long way away. But it feels as though you're already behind in life, and getting farther behind with every day that passes.

Or perhaps you have started a family. You had a picturesque wedding, replete with sparkling grape juice in glasses called "flutes," which were formerly known to you only as instruments played mostly by girls and the really weird guy in junior high band. You have been blessed with 2.2 children. You love your spouse, and your spouse loves you, but the two of you are so busy that you barely see each other, and when you do, you're so exhausted that you barely talk. It feels as if life has become a series of overloaded five-day stretches, bookended by tornado-like weekends crammed with Little League, Powderpuffs, youth group, church, and lawn mowing—and before you blink, it's all over. It's 5:45 a.m. on Monday, and time to start the whole thing again.

Week after week after week.

You didn't start out this way, but now you find yourself day-dreaming of Caribbean beaches and WaveRunners and *getting away*. Meanwhile, your kids are upstairs watching *SportsCenter* and *Keeping Up with the Kardashians* or worse in their rooms, and you just can't really dredge up the desire to interact with them. Your family is *getting away*—from you—and you know it, but you feel powerless to change it. Middle age has struck—or perhaps it is now a thing of the past—but it still doesn't seem that you have ever really gotten over the hump.

It feels like you're up on the rock, and you're stuck.

IN SEARCH OF ENCOURAGEMENT

Many Christians today, I think, go to church because of situations like these, hoping for help from the church. The pastoral staff work hard, they're likable, and they want the people to know God. There are abundant activities and numerous programs to plug into. The sermons are practical and under-standable. These messages offer guidance from the Bible and help for those in need. It's all very safe and well-intentioned, because in general, the church goes out of its way to *not offend*. It doesn't ask you to become some sort of spiritual superstar. It meets you where you are, which you like, but when you actually think about it, you sometimes wonder whether you're growing in your faith.

So you don't want to be stuck, and your church doesn't want you to either. But somehow, despite the practical sermons and how-to guidance, things don't really get fixed.

The needle doesn't move.

Something has happened to many of us today. We're not sure what transpired to make it so. We just know that we're a little off. We love the Lord, and we want to love him more, but we don't really know how to ramp everything up. We feel a variety of things, but they boil down to a mixture of fear, uncertainty, and boredom. And what does all this mean for our actual, day-to-day lives? It means, I think, that at the base, we fear making the wrong decision, taking the wrong step. We know God is good and real, but we struggle to act on that belief in everyday life, because our problems feel bigger than God's promises.

This directly affects our faith. It leads us, whether we're aware of it or not, to a play-it-safe mentality. We want to sit back, steer clear of scary circumstances, and generally get through the challenges before us. We don't want to call attention to ourselves, to feel cultural sting because of our Christianity, or to risk shaking our lives up.

It would be great, we think, for life to be as calm and quiet and manageable and low-stress as possible. Just put your head down and get through the day. Don't ruffle feathers; don't alienate friends because of your faith; don't risk being branded as a hateful evangelical. We find ourselves like kids in elementary school whose teacher woke up grumpy (and we've all been there): as believers, we're just trying to fly beneath the radar, not expose ourselves, and stay intact until the bell rings.

If this sounds like you at all, I know how you feel. I've felt many of these things myself. I have college loans. I have two young kids to care for. Some days my future seems altogether unclear, and this can leave me feeling a lack of boldness, on my heels, unsure of what to do next in a big, bad world that wants to swallow me (or so it appears).

Life is not easy. All of us know this personally. Don't get me wrong; I'm not suffering at this point in time in terrible ways. But I would be lying if I said that providing for a young family, giving my family my all when I get home, being involved at church, and trying to mentor students isn't taxing. It is. And if I let the busyness of my life get to me, I catch myself wishing for things to just calm down and get *easy*.

But that's not really the way it's supposed to be for godly adults. I know that; it's just that I'm tempted by my flesh to think I'm owed some kind of fantasy life with no stress and no responsibility.

We come from different backgrounds, and our struggles take different forms, but many of us today encounter these pressures. In such cases, we find ourselves wanting more than to merely avoid cultural shame. In the face of our personal challenges, we feel like *opting out*, just getting away from the whole thing.

Forget trying to avoid the grumpy teacher. We're looking to bolt the class.

And you know what? This is what many people in our culture, in our world, are doing. Think about marriage. When your spouse grates on you, and he or she doesn't seem to make an effort to care for you in meaningful ways, and you find yourself wondering whether you've fallen out of love, what does our culture encourage us to do? Opt out. The love has died. The light has gone out. Time to move on and start over.

A writer named Judy Wachs voiced this mind-set in a poignant essay. After Wachs's husband had an affair, the couple stayed together for a chunk of time before Wachs moved apart. As she put it in the *New York Times*:

> With four children to care for, we shared the homework, car pools, tantrums and fun. So often, we congratulated each other for staying together, for finding the sweet spot that was always there.
>
> And when I finally left our marriage after 22 years, not for another man but to strike out on my own, he showed me the same empathy and understanding that I had shown him more than a decade before. Instead of parting with acrimony, we were able to move on with love, tenderness and great memories. He eventually found a new woman to love and marry, and I now consider her among my closest friends.[3]

Many Christians believe that Jesus allows divorce in cases of adultery (Matt. 5:32; 19:9). That technical biblical issue, though, is not what I'm concerned with here.

What troubles me most is not that divorce happened in this case, but the *manner* in which it happened. The reason for the dissolution of this bond seems to have been rooted in an emotion, not a conviction. Wachs seems to have just moved on, drifted away, cast herself off. The bond of marriage worked for a while, and then it dissolved into thin air, with little explanation, little rationale, and seemingly little work in later years to do the most impressive and Christlike thing and *stay together.*

If we allow it to take hold of us, this mind-set will apply not simply to marriage, but to all of life. When our fundamental bonds are weakened, others will fracture too. We'll jump from church to church; we'll move from friend to friend; we'll shift from job to job. Most significantly, we'll find our faith flickering. Our devotion to God will be shaky. Our desire to sacrifice comfort and convenience and acceptance will overwhelm our faith. We'll stop putting it on the line for Christ.

We'll find ourselves in search of encouragement and deep connection, but with few pathways by which to get there.

WORKING AGAINST OURSELVES: THE PROBLEM OF SIN

We thought life was supposed to be different for believers. But it's actually pretty tough. What's going on here?

Part of what's happened, I think, is that in our culture, accustomed as many of us are to ease and happiness and comfort and ever-increasing mobility, we've missed that life is actually going to be tough in a fallen world. We think that if we're doing things right and hitting our marks with God, we should be firing on all cylinders. Our hopes should be met. Our stocks—real and metaphorical—should climb.

But in reality, as we've pointed out, persecution exists. Work is long. Marriages feel real pressure. It's hard to be single when you don't want to be. Church life can feel like it's stuck in neutral. We could go on. It's not inhuman or sub-spiritual to admit these things—it's actually really good, and what the author of Ecclesiastes did at length.

So, yes, we need to remember that, well, life is hard. Comfort and ease and security for many of us can be fleeting. This is what life in a fallen world looks like, and to be entirely honest, this is what it means to be a fallen person. We will be afraid when we shouldn't (John 6:16–20). We will be racked with anxiety when we needn't be (Phil. 4:6). We will avoid being bold when we should be, to avoid shaming (Matt. 5:11–12). We'll be unkind to our family members (Eph. 6:4). Our churches might offer us "milk" and not "meat," fluffy teaching that doesn't mature us, but we won't always take steps to pursue maturity ourselves (Heb. 5:11–14 KJV).

In different ways, as we can see, many of us struggle to trust in the goodness of God. Because of this, we find ourselves living life without the sense of purpose and courage that the gospel creates in us.

HUNKER DOWN TO LIVE FEARFULLY

All of the foregoing means we end up living life a certain way. There are two major patterns that result from a defeated Christian faith that is real but not vibrant.

First, we stop living aggressively for the Lord. Each of us can perhaps remember a time when our faith thrived. Maybe we were in a great church, or around really strong Christian friends.

We had Bible study seemingly around the clock; we prayed what now seems like all the time. Our faith was soaring.

I had one of these experiences. Many Christians do. It was during college. In my sophomore year, I started meeting almost nightly with three to five other believers. This was not at a spiritual powerhouse; we were at Bowdoin College, an academically tough, secular, New England school in beautiful Brunswick, Maine, founded to train Congregationalist pastors. When I was there, fewer than thirty Christians attended the weekly InterVarsity Christian Fellowship meetings. This out of an enrollment of sixteen hundred. We did not know of a single evangelical faculty member, or at least one who would publicly identify as such. And yet, it was in this context that the Lord got ahold of my heart.

Before the Lord worked dramatically in my life, I was, like many of my peers, sports-crazed. I lived for sports. That's what I watched, talked about, played on the computer, played in real life, and thought about. Church? I went to it. God? I believed in him and generally followed him.

But sold-out Christian? Hmm . . . not so much.

Everything changed when I was cut from the basketball team in the fall. I crashed emotionally. Following a frustrating high school career—after two years of varsity basketball, I hesitate to call it a career, but hey, it's my book—I had wanted to prove to myself and my hometown that I could make it. I wanted more than anything else to *be* a player. It was an identity issue. Here I was, going to a great school that could advance my learning in remarkable ways, and all I wanted to do was make a basketball team.

This is what happens, my friends, when your priorities are out of whack, when the gospel, and the great God who has given it to us, isn't your focus. You make small things your center. You lose sight of what truly matters. And whether you succeed or fail in your lesser pursuits, you get lost.

I showed up to Thursday night Bible study that same week at the local Baptist church, urged to go by my godly roommate. There I heard about blind Bartimaeus crying out to Christ for sight. I realized that I was like him. I had no hope outside of Jesus. No one else was coming along to save me and bless me.

This was it. Outside of Jesus, there was no other train coming to the station to my rescue. So I prayed for God to transform me. And that's what happened. That's how my friends and I ended up spending hours in prayer and Bible study on a chilly New England college campus, when we could have been studying. We were hungry for truth. We had fallen in love with an awesome God. We wanted more of him, and less of ourselves and this world.

But seasons like this do not always last. When they subside, they can be very hard—impossible, even—to reclaim. When friends go on their way, you graduate, people go to a different church, or whatever else, your spiritual vitality can ebb. You don't plan for that to happen. It just does.

Maybe that's where you find yourself. I've certainly seen, now that I'm older and busier, that it's much harder to set aside time for communion with the Lord. I'm not *trying* to grow distant from him. It can just happen, if I let it. Perhaps that resonates with you.

When we see our vitality slip, a switch flips. We stop working hard at the daily discipline of godliness. We're building a young career in a fast-paced city, and that consumes us. We go days without reading God's Word. We're finishing a tough degree program, and without knowing what's happening, we end up buried in our books, barely coming up for air. We're not seeking to avoid the Bible or prayer or church. It just happens. And slowly, quietly, the strength of our faith wanes. We begin compromising morally, watching stuff we shouldn't, doing stuff we shouldn't, talking about unedifying things. We lose our nerve to witness and live a bold life, because deep down we know that we're not backing up our talk. We may continue to be aggressive about certain things—careers or the pursuit of money or degrees or friends or having fun—but not about what matters most: the Lord. Worshipping our Trinitarian God. Delighting ourselves in him.

So we stop living boldly for God. We risk our piety to indulge our sin. Without knowing it, perhaps, we've made a bad bargain.

And we'll be the ones who feel the consequences.

Second, we gradually lose enthusiasm for building godly things. Along with the problem I've just outlined is a closely related one. When you start tuning out spiritually and you stop living aggressively for Jesus in your own private life, everything around you will suffer.

What do I mean? Well, if you're not thriving in your walk with Christ, you're not going to be in a position to help others thrive, are you?

Do you see this? Do you feel it? I think many people do nowadays. We know it'd be better to be building something great. We're well aware that there is a lot of gospel work to do, no matter what fields we're in. We understand that God has given us certain talents and roles and opportunities to use for his glory. But we don't have the zeal necessary to pull off the work.

We can see where we should be. We just don't really have the oomph, the spiritual horsepower, to get there.

And so we shift into maintenance mode. You know the

difference between, say, a restaurant that strives for excellence, and one that's content to serve an average product? That applies to us. We settle for average. Our marriages are okay. Our kids are fine. Our church—well, it's getting along. We're not setting new benchmarks for Christian laborers in our jobs, but we're doing what we need to do. Sometimes we pray. Occasionally we read the Bible. Once in a while we talk with someone about the Lord. But it's all very maintenance-y. Ordinary. Without zip.

This is decaf faith. And that means the people around us, those we should lead and influence to live on mission for the living Messiah, who reigns in heaven, live decaf lives. They may not be crashing and burning, but they're not soaring, either, because we're not building something big.

THERE IS AMAZING HOPE, THOUGH, FOR YOU

To this point, we have covered some tough stuff. We've seen that many of us are feeling heat these days. We're facing a variety of social and economic challenges. We may not be built up at church. Perhaps we're sliding in sin. And it's possible, consequently, that we are slipping in our walks with God. Because of that, we might not be blessing those around us as they need, and as we want.

All this diagnosis of what many Christians are facing is not born of despair, though. We've got to see what's troubling so many of us before we can fix the problem. In general, we're not feeling aggressive today. We're fearful. We're not thriving. We're on our heels.

We need to be on our toes.

But our faith doesn't have the electrical current it needs. So many of us are battened down. We're unassertive. We're unsure. We need help.

We may find ourselves discouraged by our circumstances. But Scripture has impossibly good news for people like you and me, news that will shake us up and leave us transformed. Here's the trick, though: this good news is not, contrary to what you may have heard, that life can be magically cured of any challenges. It's not the absence of struggle or stress that the Bible promises us. God wants to give us something better than that. In spite of whatever this world throws at us, whatever obstacles loom large in our hearts or our circumstances, God promises that he will give us the ultimate gift: *his unending presence and love*. This is better than any financial achievement, social triumph, or physical transformation.

Flowing from this is a second gift: a purposeful life devoted to promoting his gospel in whatever roles we're called to play so he can be maximally glorified.

These two gifts are what we'll be exploring in pages ahead.

CONCLUSION: WHY YOU SHOULD JUMP OFF THE ROCK

So maybe you're with me to this point. You agree that life for many of us is not as we would want it to be. You want to grow in your faith. You want to see your friends, family members, and church thrive in the Lord. You want something better, bigger, bolder. The good news is, that kind of life exists. It's here. It's right in front of you.

In the next chapter, we'll zero in like a laser on just how much God wants us to trust him and exercise faith in him. We'll see that though we may feel that inspiration is lacking, it's actually close at hand. Hope, real and tangible, is by our side. It's found in obedience. There's no uncertainty in the goodness of this direction. It's right there before us.

So you're standing on the rock. You're looking out at what could be. You see where you want to go.

Now all you have to do is jump.

2 RISKY FAITH: THE CALL TO RISK

Christians today like to play it safe. We want to put ourselves in situations where we are safe "even if there is no God."

—FRANCIS CHAN, *Crazy Love*

A FEW YEARS AGO, A VERY WEIRD SERIES OF VIDEOS made their way around the web. I don't think I knew the phrase "viral video" in 2006, but this strange YouTube production fit the category long before "Gangnam Style" became the first billion-viewed YouTube clip.[1]

The videos, produced by Vintage21 Church in Raleigh, North Carolina, were based on clips from an old film about Jesus. In one of the videos, the character of Jesus stands in a temple and says in a nasal voice:

"Hello. Welcome to the first Christian church. Greetings.

"Here are the rules.

"Rule number 1: Spend all of your free time in church.

"Rule number 2: You're not allowed to have any fun unless you're laughing at how dumb the devil is.

"Rule number 3: Wear T-shirts with my face on it.

"Rule number 4: Always smile and act happy."[2]

Whether or not one appreciates or finds humor in these videos, they certainly made me think. Was Jesus a frail, fragile person? What was the fundamental purpose of his mission on earth—was it to hand down a bunch of rules? Did he come to outlaw "fun" and to force believers to do little but go to church and sit there, glazed-eyed, looking happy?

I don't think many people would actually answer yes to the questions I've just posed. But there is something to the strange portrait of the Savior found in the Vintage21 series, something I think is quite important. The videos portray faith as many people conceive it, as a protective reality. You know Jesus and want to follow him? Then hunker down, get out of the stormy elements of this world, and huddle with fellow religious types who want to "always smile and act happy."

Life as many evangelicals approach it isn't supposed to be scary. We talked about this in chapter 1. Many of us see the challenges before us and want God to make everything easy. We want the Jesus of our best life now to give us a blanket and some hot cocoa, not send us out into a fearsome world. But the Vintage21 Jesus series points us the opposite way. It seems to be arguing that in American culture, we have fundamentally misrepresented Jesus.

We have domesticated him and left him a pale and weak reflection of himself.

The Jesus of Scripture is radically different from this Messiah of our own imagining. In the pages that follow, we will sketch a portrait of the strength and boldness of the true God. We will do so by zeroing in on the parable of the talents, an often-overlooked message of Christ. This parable shows us that godly faith does not shy away from God-oriented risk, but embraces it.

Here's the major point we are going to see in this chapter:

God doesn't want his people to be fearful, but faithful. He's not trying to cool us down, but to heat us up. Yet, biblical faith isn't reckless or careless. It is trusting, confident, and fearless *because* it is grounded in almighty God.

READ A LITTLE DEEPER . . .

I don't know if you've read or watched *Gulliver's Travels* recently. I would guess that for a fair number of us, this book fits in the category of "Books We Should Have Read (but Haven't) and Yet Still Nod Knowingly About When Referenced in Conversation."

I actually did read the book, lo, those many years ago. *Gulliver's Travels* appealed to me on the level that I am guessing it appealed to many folks: it was a fantastic tale, a story of tiny people and world travel and the unfortunate feats of Gulliver. How surprising, then, to learn later that the book by Jonathan Swift was actually a work of political satire. Scholars debate the exact thesis, but many agree that the book makes a broader point about the silliness of nineteenth-century European politics.

Enough literary nerdery, though. This is true of so much of the material we read, right? Many of us realize that when we're reading Tolkien, for example, there's a broader message beyond the Orcs and Ents and Really, Really, Really Long Songs by Tom Bombadil. But you know what's striking? When it comes to the Bible, we don't always read it as carefully as we do other texts. We read it for its plain meaning, which is right and good. But if we don't treat the Bible with care, we can miss certain truths and ideas that are right before our eyes.

This is true of a passage you've likely read before but won't hear expounded at many evangelical mega-conferences. Matthew 25:14–30 is a seemingly straightforward swath of scripture. Let's read it.

Speaking of the last days, Jesus says:

For it will be like a man going on a journey, who called his servants and entrusted to them his property. To one he gave five talents, to another two, to another one, to each according to his ability. Then he went away. He who had received the five talents went at once and traded with them, and he made five talents more. So also he who had the two talents made two talents more. But he who had received the one talent went and dug in the ground and hid his master's money. Now after a long time the master of those servants came and settled accounts with them. And he who had received the five talents came forward, bringing five talents more, saying, "Master, you delivered to me five talents; here I have made five talents more." His master said to him, "Well done, good and faithful servant. You have been faithful over a little; I will set you over much. Enter into the joy of your master." And he also who had the two talents came forward, saying, "Master, you delivered to me two talents; here I have made two talents more." His master said to him, "Well done, good and faithful servant. You have been faithful over a little; I will set you over much. Enter into the joy of your master."

The parable to this point is pretty direct. It makes a lot of sense. If you are faithful to God, it seems, he will bless you. Most often when this parable is cited or preached about, it's this helpful lesson that is emphasized.

Things get serious in the final part of the passage:

He also who had received the one talent came forward, saying, "Master, I knew you to be a hard man, reaping where you
did not sow, and gathering where you scattered no seed, so
I was afraid, and I went and hid your talent in the ground.
Here you have what is yours." But his master answered him,
"You wicked and slothful servant! You knew that I reap where
I have not sown and gather where I scattered no seed? Then
you ought to have invested my money with the bankers, and
at my coming I should have received what was my own with
interest. So take the talent from him and give it to him who
has the ten talents. For to everyone who has will more be
given, and he will have an abundance. But from the one who
has not, even what he has will be taken away. And cast the
worthless servant into the outer darkness. In that place there
will be weeping and gnashing of teeth."

As is immediately clear, the parable closes on a hair-raising
note (as it does in the parallel text, Luke 19:12–28). If we are not
fruitful servants, we learn, we will face eternal consequences.
How, then, do most of us walk away from this text? We find ourselves rightly resolved to steward our resources well. We want
to invest our own "talents" rightly (an individual talent from
this era would have been worth around sixty thousand dollars in
modern markets, by the way). And quite appropriately, we come
away from this passage wanting badly to be faithful servants and
not "wicked and slothful" people.

This is the major application of the passage drawn by basically every commentator I've looked at (including many of my

favorite New Testament scholars). Some of them make mention of the importance of trusting faith and unwearying commitment to Christ, but for many, the real heart of this parable boils down to money and stewardship. Here's an example from a popular commentary dealing with the parable:

> One of the first lessons that I learned a few years ago that really changed the way I thought about money was that none of it is mine. It is all God's. I have the privilege and opportunity to be a steward of what He has given me.
>
> Once I began looking at my money this way, it changed my whole financial outlook and helped me to be more focused on pleasing God with the money entrusted to me.[3]

None of this is false. These are good and true teachings. But I think there's much more here. The parable of the talents is not simply a call to wise management of our lives, as even many robust evangelical resources argue.

Nothing less than a way to live is outlined in Jesus' parable.

It's like a story I read recently. A Wisconsin couple invited a furniture appraiser to their home to look over some antique furniture they wanted to sell. The appraiser happened to be an art prospector as well. Working his way through the elderly couple's home, he came across a painting that caught his attention. It looked, rather surprisingly, like a Van Gogh. *Can't be*, he thought. But it was. Furthermore, this was no "mere" Van Gogh. It was the *Still Life with Flowers*, now a treasured part of the artist's body of work. It gets better though: no one knew it was a masterpiece.

Until, that is, the appraiser walked into the home, spotted

the painting offhand, and identified an original Van Gogh worth $1.4 million.[4]

Not a bad day in real estate, eh?

WHEN A PARABLE IS NOT JUST A PARABLE, BUT A WAY OF LIFE

I submit to you, dear reader, that we have stumbled across a scriptural Van Gogh. Do you see it? Did it sneak up on you, as it did me?

This passage, as we noted, takes a surprising turn. First the "master," upon returning home, blesses the faithful servants. Then, in a twist that takes our breath away, Jesus curses the unworthy servant who does not invest his "talent" but instead hunkers down, avoiding the hardship and pain of this fallen world.

But wait a minute—wasn't the "wicked and slothful" servant merely accepting life in a fallen world? Wasn't he rightly aware of the sinfulness of this realm, all the darkness and hurt and pain it causes those who stick their necks out? He was "afraid," it seems to me, in a way that you and I can understand. He found himself in a dark place and a scary world. All the forces of evil seemed arrayed against him.

We can feel just this way too. As we discussed in chapter 1, life in our modern age seems to come at us with secular ferocity. Cherished social institutions seem to be crumbling before our eyes. The wind of popular opinion reverses course on us and attacks evangelicals for believing in traditional marriage. Life just seems hard, whether financially or domestically.

In these kinds of circumstances, you and I can find ourselves afraid. On our heels. So we can be tempted—easily tempted—to act as the final servant did. He was afraid. He knew in a lackadaisical way that God would do what he wanted—that he would be "reaping where [none] sowed"—so he decided to sit the whole thing out. How many of us, encountering this scenario, would make the same choice? If we're honest, I think many of us might.

Perhaps we *are* making this kind of choice in our everyday lives. We're hunkered down.

Here is what we see, though, when we really burrow into this spiritually profound parable. The problem with the wicked servant is not simply that he didn't invest his talent. It is this: *he didn't want to risk*. He wanted to be safe. He preferred that life be quiet. He didn't care to engage in some Cosmic Struggle for Righteousness. He'd rather tune out and drop out, and then have his ticket punched in the end.

It wasn't that he was dumb; he knew the master would return, just as we know Jesus will come again (1 Thess. 4:16–17). He just thought he was playing the game expertly, getting to lead a comfortable, safe, risk-free life now. Then, when it was over, because he had been appropriately religious, he could live with God forever.

But Jesus' response to this way of life is positively stunning. He denounces the man: "You wicked and slothful servant!" This really is as strong a condemnation as it sounds. The word for "wicked," *achreios*, indicates something that is utterly without value. But why is the servant so wicked? Because he did not trust God. As we talked about in chapter 1, he did not remember the central truth about God: he is good. The master, as Jesus set forth in this parable, is good. If the servant knew that his master was great, Jesus says to him, "Then you ought to have invested my money with the bankers, and at my coming I should have received what was my own with interest."

There you have it. This is our Van Gogh moment, albeit one staring us in the face. Jesus is not simply telling us through this parable to be "good stewards." He is doing that, but more. He is giving us divine insight into the best way to live in this world. The darkness seems great, life is hard, and the time is short, but true followers of the master—of God—are not to bury their heads in the sand, because God is in control. The wicked servant did bury his head. But believers are supposed to find incredible, world-shaking confidence in God. This "Master" is indeed able to do wonders, as the foolish man thought. But this is not supposed to paralyze us. It is supposed to create a life of boldness and faith and action and *risk*.

We can boil it down to this: *God's awesomeness should propel our faithfulness.*

If our fundamental calculus in life is safety, we've misunderstood the Bible. John Piper recently published a short book that got straight to the point: *Risk Is Right.*[5] God doesn't save us to coddle us. He doesn't give the gift of his beloved Son so we can hide away, safe and secure from a sinful world and all its challenges, like the wicked servant. God makes us his own so he can unleash us to be vessels of mercy. He saves you, my friend, to make you a comet in the sky, a vessel of righteousness, a citizen of the kingdom, a priest to God, a faithful and fearless worker in his vineyard.

So you and I are worried that we might miss God's will. Here's the incredible truth: we already know God's will for our lives. We are saved not so we can hedge our bets. We are saved to put everything on the table for God. The calculus, the fundamental orientation, of every second we live is toward risk for God. Just like the faithful servants—those who had five and two talents—we're to get to work, to seek to make more, to spread the gospel. The Master *is* good, impossibly good, and he delights to reward his children (Matt. 7:11).

All this is good and exciting and meaningful. The wicked servant saw the power of God and misunderstood it. He thought God's greatness was life-taking. In truth, God's sovereignty is life-*giving*. We're saved to plunge headlong into a life of God-inspired, Christ-centered, gospel-driven risk. We don't know when the Master is returning; we don't know what may come of our efforts. We're not guaranteed any earthly results.

But we are called to work while there is still time.

IT'S OKAY—GOD *WANTS YOU* TO *RISK*!

The parable of the talents is a bombshell. It's a window into the heart of true Christianity. It shows you what your life is supposed to look like. You could use many words to summarize it, but fundamentally, you are called by God to live a life of *bold faith*. God *wants* you to risk.

Living a life of gospel risk doesn't mean running like a dog chasing a cat, ears flattened against your skull, after the first half-sane spiritual idea that pops into your mind. We must be careful, thoughtful Christians who aren't afraid to seek guidance from wise friends in the faith. Proverbs 11:14 is right: "In an abundance of counselors there is safety." We must also pray for wisdom and direction even as the apostles did. As just one example, when it came time to appoint a successor to the disgraced and deceased Judas, the apostles first prayed to God for wisdom about who to select in his place (Acts 1:12–26). Then they acted in response to that prayer, trusting that God would guide them, and that he would be honored by their trusting action.

That is a pattern we must follow as well, over and over and over again in our lives. Prayerfully, reflectively, and as wisely as you can through scriptural study and counsel from church members and leaders, you forge your strategy for using the life God has given you for his glory. Then you step up. In a phrase, you put it all on the line.

You risk.

Don't miss this. You may have been trained as many believers are in mystical, fearful Christianity. If so, the Bible has great news for you. Provided you are saturating your mind and your prayers with biblical wisdom in a Romans 12:1–2 sense—such that your heart and mind are being transformed by Scripture—it's appropriate to strategize, and plan, and then to *act*.

This means *not* living fearfully. It means we prayerfully consider how to strengthen our families, and then we act. It means we take control of our spiritual lives, and we commit by God's grace to that Bible reading plan we've put off. It means we stop excusing our lack of exercise and our poor health and propel ourselves toward physical fitness. It means we speak up when we have a chance to share the gospel, or speak biblical truth, or call out corruption and unfairness in our workplace.

So it is for we who labor for the gospel, the ultimate "talent," the pearl of great price. Our chief joy and call in life as believers—no matter what we do on a daily basis—is to speak and live in such a way as to advance the gospel so people are saved and transformed by Christ. We store up "crowns" and "treasures" in heaven when we respond to God's call to obedience and courage, even though God is the one who gives us the grace to do so (see 2 Tim. 4:8; Matt. 6:20; Phil. 2:13).

Praise God for this risk-empowering equation!

JESUS CAME TO EMBOLDEN US

A 2009 article in *Newsweek* made a noteworthy point: stress, contrary to what we sometimes think, is not necessarily bad for us. Some stress is actually good for us, according to author Mary Carmichael: "In the short term, it can energize us, 'revving up our systems to handle what we have to handle,' says Judith Orloff, a psychiatrist at UCLA. In the long term, stress can motivate us to do better at jobs we care about. A little of it can prepare us for a lot later on, making us more resilient."[6]

According to medical experts, if we experience too much stress, we become great candidates for a heart attack. Too little, though, and we may end up a puddle on the floor. Just the right amount aimed at a truly meaningful goal is actually really good for you. That's true spiritually as well as physically.

It's not the *absence* of any challenge that will invigorate your life and mine; it's the *presence* of the right one.

This fits elegantly with the testimony of Scripture. Think of the apostle Paul, soon to die. Writing his disciple Timothy, a young pastor and leader of God's people, he said these inspiring words: "I remind you to fan into flame the gift of God, which is in you through the laying on of my hands, for God gave us a spirit not of fear but of power and love and self-control" (2 Tim. 1:6–7). It wasn't simply a lack of conflict that would smooth Timothy's way. It was the knowledge of the power of God in him. Timothy was fighting the good fight against false teachers. He didn't need to damp down his witness, to soften his tone. What he needed to do was stay in the fight, trusting in God's power as he did.

This speaks to our situation, too, whether or not we're pastors. Every Christian faces his or her own unique situations and trials. They do not happen by accident. They are a part of how God grows us and uses us. The life God gives to his children is not meek and mild. It is bold and captivating. The Lord does not obliterate everyday existence, but rather transforms it by bringing us into his work. The life we now lead, therefore, is anything but ordinary, much as it may seem otherwise. The Lord wants to shake us up and get us on mission for him. This will mean embracing the call to follow God no matter what circumstances we face.

This is a pattern with the triune God. The Father grants us perfect peace (Isa. 26:3), but he does so by *disturbing* our serenity, our natural order. He doesn't call us to himself and throw a blanket on us so we can take a long Christian nap and wake up in heaven. We're like Lazarus from John 11. Once, we were dead in sin, but now God calls us to wake up.

Jesus came to embolden us, not to anesthetize us. This is true of God all throughout the Bible. You read the Bible back through to understand God's character, and he will surprise you. He wrestled with Jacob, putting him in a divine headlock, to cement his covenant with the man. He had Joseph kidnapped by his brothers (thus fulfilling the dreams of countless older siblings), thrown into a pit, and then packaged off to Egypt, all to save Israel during a ferocious famine to come. Moses didn't lead Israel from a throne, with palmetto branches cooling his tan skin, but marched them through a desert, only to drop dead at the end. David was called out of shepherding not merely to fight in a great war, but to challenge a humongous warrior whose spear was taller than most men. The call of God often causes drama. It's a sacrificial call, not a self-serving one. And it transforms us, but not in the neat and comfortable way we might expect.

You follow God, and you just might get asked to walk in the wilderness. For forty years.

This doesn't let up in Scripture. When you come to the prophetic books, you see God asking prophets to lie on their sides for months at a time, wailing for his people. Following Yahweh did not mean ease and security (in an earthly sense) for Isaiah and Jeremiah; it meant pain and hardship and even frustration with God's people. When Jesus took up his ministry, he turned over tables, hunted down demons, and disturbed Lazarus from his deathly sleep. Paul got knocked down on the Damascus road, was essentially kidnapped by the Lord, and then underwent continual hardship while preaching the gospel. Most of the apostles were martyred for their faith.

Your cushiest life now, eh?

YOU DON'T UNSUBSCRIBE FROM JESUS

What does all of this add up to? Well, when God comes your way, he calls you to risk it all on his behalf.

He doesn't ask you to sign a box indicating you prefer him

over other religious options. Following the ruler of all things doesn't equal joining an e-mail list. I think we're tempted to conceive of biblical faith in this manner. You subscribe, get some messages in your inbox, distractedly scan them, and then go about the serious business of your day. Sure, you're signed up for the Jesus Is My Lord e-mail list, but it doesn't affect your life in any crazy way. It's another message to check, right alongside your forty weekly e-mails from J. Crew, your Facebook notifications ("Belinda McCarthy has sent you 750,000 cows on Farmville!"), and your fantasy football updates.

Jesus is not an e-mail list.

Everyone Christ calls, he puts in the same kind of situation we've just mentioned from Scripture. Think of how he summoned his disciples. He didn't encourage them to put an "I'm for Jesus" sticker on their fishing boats. He appeared basically out of nowhere. He startled them. He stunned them. And he immediately offered them a choice: follow me and leave everything, or don't. This is it. Your chance is now. You are, in this moment, going to have to lay down your fishing nets, and that's that.

This is exactly what happened in Matthew's Gospel:

> While walking by the Sea of Galilee, [Jesus] saw two brothers, Simon (who is called Peter) and Andrew his brother, casting a net into the sea, for they were fishermen. And he said to them, "Follow me, and I will make you fishers of men." Immediately they left their nets and followed him. And going on from there he saw two other brothers, James the son of Zebedee and John his brother, in the boat with Zebedee their father, mending their nets, and he called them. Immediately they left the boat and their father and followed him. (4:18–22)

You see this, right? It can't be any more stark. One minute these men were fishing and mending nets; the next they were following the Messiah-King, Jesus Christ, having been drafted into the most important mission in the history of humankind.

Now, let's be clear: these men were called to unique roles. They were Christ's apostles. You and I will not become apostles. That was a special office for a certain time. But we are all called to make a clear choice with eternal implications: either we put it all on the line for Jesus and his gospel, or we refuse the fullness of God's kindness and continue serving Satan and being slowly drained of life by him.

That's what following Jesus means. That's what risking everything for the gospel looks like.

THE WAY OF CHRIST IS NOT NECESSARILY EASY, BUT IT MAY BE ORDINARY

The biblical leaders we've looked at thus far lived outsized, unordinary lives. They had wild dreams. They took on emperors. They performed and witnessed miracles.

But what about you and me? Is our faith weak compared to theirs? How are we supposed to match up? Think about it:

We have deadlines, not a world empire, to conquer.

We don't have lions after us; we've got babies and toddlers to feed.

We're not casting out demons; we're attacking papers and quizzes instead.

So are we supposed to overhaul everything? What does it mean *today* when Jesus says to us, through his Word, "Follow me"?

Well, my modern friends, we're not supposed to re-create some prior age, some halcyon era in a faraway kingdom. We're called to be faithful in our day and our own context.

We'll talk more about this in coming chapters. But our risk on behalf of the gospel is deeply meaningful.

Whether you're overseas or in your backyard, your sacrifices for Christ are intensely important. When we give up dreams of ease and quiet and lack of suffering for Christ, God gets glory. Gospel risk has entered the equation.

In this way, you and I can emulate the great heroes of the Bible. We shouldn't read their stories with shame, as if we can't measure up to them. We should see them as ordinary people God used to do great things in his name. That's what we are called to do in our life situations. We submit ourselves entirely to God's will, knowing that his gospel is true and our lives are hidden in him, and we ask him to use us. All of us. Wherever we are, whatever we do.

I remember what this meant for me when my God-given faith really hit its boiling point. I was in college, and the Lord had called me to serve him. Did I know exactly what that meant? I didn't have a clue, really. But my ambition, my honest desire, was to serve him to the fullest of my ability in whatever field he opened to me. Because of the grace of God activated in my heart, I was good to go.

Has this always meant that it's clear what I should do? No. It has not. Committing your entire life to the Lord of the cosmos is not predictable. Sometimes, frankly, it's challenging. The life of faith, even ambitious faith, is really the life of trust. This means waiting. Praying hard. Seeking wisdom. Even if you launch a big plan for your life by which you want to promote

God's glory with all your being (as I hope you will!), you will find that there is still a great deal of waiting, and trusting, and praying, and fighting anxiety, and killing envy, and staying in your lane.

You don't always know what's coming; in fact, you usually don't.

I'll be totally honest here: I'm not great at waiting. I want the whole plan now. Maybe you're like me. How do the pieces of my life fit in place? Where am I supposed to be investing? *Am I getting it all wrong?* This is a line of thinking that comes from my sinful heart. Satan uses it sometimes to tempt me to doubt God's good plan, and the ordinariness of my life seems to confirm those doubts. *If I was really getting after it, I'd be doing X.*

But this is all wrong, sinfully wrong. Yes, I'm willing and even eager to drop everything for the Lord. But a commitment to gospel risk doesn't mean a predefined course of action. It means you're willing to do whatever the Lord wants and makes clear for you. You're no longer pursuing ease and comfort and fun and hedonism and emptiness as your goal. It's all about the Lord, and wholeheartedly serving him wherever you're called to be.

This may mean, as we'll see, leaving your country to take the gospel to an unreached people group. That would be great! Or it may mean being a secretary in a small town, a phone salesperson in a suburban mall, a mother to two tiny kids in a massive city, or a thousand other scenarios. When we follow Jesus as the apostles did, we have no idea how he will use us. He may maximize his glory through us by a faithful but nonetheless "normal" existence. Or he may have a more unusual route of glorification.

No matter what you do on a daily basis, you can rest in this: your walk may not be predictable, but it will be transformative and full of grace, and powered by joy that cuts through all the lesser things of this world, leaving you to savor the mercy and power of God shown you and made your own through the cross and empty tomb. When Christ is your all, and you're living for him, then you're in God's will.

Period.

So yes, you and I will battle sin and doubt. But I hope you see that in the end, this isn't a fair fight. Sin can't win when measured against God. Whatever your call and vocation, the terms of "counting the cost" (see Luke 15:25–35) and "following Jesus" lead to the same conclusion: compared to the eternal weight of glory, this fading world doesn't have a chance. That's the truth of gospel risk. Counting the cost, and choosing God over the world and its temptations, always leaves us with the same result: it's all worth it. Christ is incomprehensibly worth it.

The world always loses. God always wins.

OUR CERTAIN SALVATION

We began by talking about a weird video about an effeminate Jesus and the insipid, cloistered way of life some think he formed. I have presented a very different picture of the Messiah and the life he intends to give us. I have suggested, all told, that we should live boldly for Christ, and that we should embrace risk in his name.

But wait, you may be thinking. *Isn't this Christianity? Isn't biblical faith supposed to be—I don't know—safe?* Let me be clear:

this is not a leap of faith in the sense that we don't know if God is trustworthy. He is absolutely trustworthy (Ps. 100:5). This is not a dangerous proposition such that your soul is in jeopardy if you follow God. He will keep you spiritually secure no matter what may happen in this life (John 10:28). Neither is this an irrational calculation to follow a well-intentioned but bumbling leader. God is in complete control, and he always does what is best for his children for the sake of his glory (Isa. 45:7). God never risks; he's never at a loss for what to do; he's absolutely sovereign, and his is a beneficent sovereignty, a good authority. The Lord is the leader we all naturally crave but have difficulty finding: he is altogether powerful, and absolutely good.

His goodness is secured for you and me by Jesus Christ, who gave his life on the cross so we could know liberation from sin and death and hell and taste the goodness of God in this life and in the perfected world to come. Jesus undertook a staggering mission, but he did so knowing that God's plan was good. He wasn't gambling for our salvation. Though the cost was high, the outcome was certain.

As we must do, Jesus trusted the Father to accomplish his plan, knowing that the Lord would restore him even as he yielded his life as a substitutionary sacrifice for sin. Think of John 17:24 (and all of John 17, really): "Father, I desire that they also, whom you have given me, may be with me where I am, to see my glory that you have given me because you loved me before the foundation of the world."

Because this was true for Christ, it is true for his people. No matter what comes our way in this fallen world, the Lord will not abandon us. David said just that in Psalm 16:10: "For you will not abandon my soul to Sheol, or let your holy one see corruption."

This was true for Jesus, and it is true for every Christian because we live in him (Eph. 2:13).

CONCLUSION

One fact remains: in responding to the parable of the talents, we really do need to give everything up. We must give up our man-made plans for worldly peace and prosperity. We must relinquish anxious management of our daily existence. We must break with a "play it safe" mentality and embrace a bigger vision of our time on this earth.

It is not our souls that should live in fear. It is our comfort, ease, quietness, boredom, fearfulness, anxiety, and sin that are in mortal danger. Christianity is not about fear. It's not about retreat. It is about advance, growth, and faith. It is about becoming someone greater in Christ than you ever thought possible.

By the Spirit's power, let's pursue that awesome goal.

3 RISKY IDENTITY: THE POWER OF THE BELIEVER

Open the eyes of my heart, Lord,
Open the eyes of my heart.

—LYRICS BY MICHAEL W. SMITH

THESE WORDS ARE FAMILIAR TO MANY WHO HAVE visited an evangelical church in recent years. They are a riff off of Psalm 119:18: "Open my eyes, that I may behold wondrous things out of your law."

When you have heard a song as popular as this one many times over, it's possible to mouth the words and not really think about them. This happens to all of us. Every so often, though, we hear a particular version of a song, and it's as if an angel has come to earth to give us that song. This is the case when you hear a twelve-year-old autistic boy named Christopher Duffley sing "Open the Eyes of My Heart."

Christopher is not your typical famous singer these days. If you have ever watched *American Idol* or *X-Factor*, then you will know what you need to be a famous vocalist: skin the color of a distressed orange, outrageous hair extensions (woman) or frosted tips (man), and the ability to continually signal your designated telephone code while the similarly orange-skinned TV host tells the audience to vote for you. Well, Christopher is different. He's an adolescent. His mother abused OxyContin while pregnant. He is autistic and blind.

Christopher has a lovely voice. But it is the passion in his singing that most stands out. When he sings of God's goodness and holiness, he abandons himself to the song. You and I sometimes struggle to remain interested in the words before us. Christopher belts them out, hitting high notes we wouldn't dare attempt. To watch him is to be simultaneously inspired, rebuked, and amazed. It is a picture of what a song can be when it is passionately felt. [1]

It is a testimony to what a twenty-six-week-old preemie baby, weighing one pound and certain to die, can become: a world-rebuking witness of God's grace.

Like so many who have overcome terrible odds, Christopher is a reminder to me of the endless hope found in God. Every person, in whatever circumstances may arise, can grow. And we all can overcome and triumph over adversity, even tremendous adversity. All of us can become something greater. The way to this growth is simple but hard to find: we need a new understanding of our identity. This is how a young man fighting major physical and situational challenges can become a vessel of God's glory. He knows he is loved and supported, and that has transformed and encouraged him.

That's also the way you and I can grow. We need to know who we are in Christ.

THE TRAGIC CASE OF THE RICH YOUNG RULER

To understand who we are in Christ, we need to see what we possess through faith in him. And to understand what we have in the gospel, I want to look at someone who had everything *but* the gospel. I want to give you, in other words, a negative example. By seeing how the "rich young ruler" turned away from Christ, you'll see the almost impossible foolishness of this decision. That will equip us, in the pages ahead, to positively see just how good the Godward life is.

Let's pick up Mark's account of this tragic figure from Mark 10:17–22:

> And as he was setting out on his journey, a man ran up and knelt before him and asked him, "Good Teacher, what must I do to inherit eternal life?" And Jesus said to him, "Why do you call me good? No one is good except God alone. You know the commandments: 'Do not murder, Do not commit adultery, Do not steal, Do not bear false witness, Do not defraud, Honor your father and mother.'" And he said to him, "Teacher, all these I have kept from my youth." And Jesus, looking at him, loved him, and said to him, "You lack one thing: go, sell all that you have and give to the poor, and you will have treasure in heaven; and come, follow me." Disheartened by the saying, he went away sorrowful, for he had great possessions.

As you can see, the rich young ruler did not want to give his all to God. He wanted "to inherit eternal life." He was willing to obey the Ten Commandments and the Mosaic Law. He didn't have a problem with religion. He was glad to make changes in his life that he liked and saw as necessary. He was clearly hungry for teaching and leadership; after all, it was he who sought out Jesus, not the other way around. He didn't merely tap Jesus on the shoulder, either. He "ran up" to the Christ, "knelt before him," and called him "Good Teacher," demonstrating that he knew that the Man before him deserved unusual honor and possessed uncommon wisdom.

So far, so good.

But this promising story takes a terrible turn at the end. Jesus offers the young man the ultimate opportunity: he can transcend this world. He can have the eternal life he seeks. It's right in front of him, in a kind of literalness that's hard to over-emphasize. Jesus, John will tell us, is "the way and the truth and the life" (John 14:6). That which the rich young ruler desires is, shockingly, before him. Humanity is and always has been obsessed with finding the path to happiness, the means to fulfillment, the way to God.

This young man is staring it—him—in the face.

But the rich young ruler is caught in a bind. He's religious, you see, but he's not truly in love with God. He hasn't banked everything on the Lord of heaven and earth. He's got one foot in and one foot out. Deep down, he's hoping against hope when he comes to the "Good Teacher" that he will be told he's doing exactly what he should be doing: "Keep it up. Stay faithful to the Ten Rules. Live a clean life. Enjoy yourself. You'll get there in the end."

But he is *not* told this. He is called to realize that he has *nothing* in the world. Everything he could ever hope to find, all he could want to become, is within reach. This is exactly what

Christ says next:

> Peter began to say to him, "See, we have left everything and
> followed you." Jesus said, "Truly, I say to you, there is no one
> who has left house or brothers or sisters or mother or father or
> children or lands, for my sake and for the gospel, who will not
> receive a hundredfold now in this time, houses and brothers
> and sisters and mothers and children and lands, with perse-
> cutions, and in the age to come eternal life. But many who are
> first will be last, and the last first." (Mark 10:28–31)

So there it is. Christians are those who have, by the sheer mercy
of God, seen that they will gain all things in God even as they lose
their worldly, sinful existence, with all its trappings. Persecution
will come; the pain of separation is inevitable; everything must
be left in the sense that nothing worldly can be worshipped any
longer. This is what Jesus was teaching in this parable: not that
material stuff is bad (though it is nothing compared to God),
but that God deserves and wants all our worship. The rich young
ruler worshiped his possessions. They were his joy.

In the end, they were his identity.

This story has tremendous significance for us as Christians.
Even after we follow Christ in faith, we will be tempted by our
sin nature to worship the things of this world. We can't lose our
salvation; we won't ultimately fall away (John 10:28). But we can
fall into our old ways of thinking. We can think that the world
offers us what we really want, and that Christianity is boring and
restrictive.

If we're not guarding our hearts, God can seem like a killjoy.

When the cost of being a believer rises (as it is and will), we can be tempted to choose the natural over the spiritual, our friends over our church, our comfort over our witness. And what does all this mean spiritually? It means we won't thrive, we won't work hard at holiness, we'll despise discipline, we'll do what comes easiest (and choose sin instead of God), and we'll see faith as an intrusion. We won't be diligent in godliness, we won't experience ongoing victory over sin, and we won't plunge into the darkness all around us to be vibrant witnesses. Instead, we'll muddle along, struggle in our personal relationships, and generally not enjoy life very much.

There is a better way. The story of the rich young ruler speaks powerfully to our situation. It calls us to go back to our roots, to remember our first love. It challenges us to take control of our hearts and to worship God with all our being.

So how can we accomplish this? How can we make a better choice?

WHAT WE CAN LEARN FROM
THIS TERRIBLE MISTAKE

It's simple: we need to learn who we are in Christ and thus what we have in him.

By seeing the incredible awfulness of the rich young ruler's decision, we are beautifully freed up to make the right one. We, in other words, are able to come face-to-face with Christ and his risky gospel, and we are able by God's lavish grace to choose rightly.

To choose Jesus.

This is who you are. A Christian is not some prettified

spiritual contestant in the great pageant of Who Can Look the Most Religious. A Christian is a person who sees that Jesus Christ and his righteousness are the needs of our heart and the apex of our satisfaction. Through the Spirit, we're able to see that Jesus is worth it all.

But here's the problem: sin does crazy things to our minds. It makes us weak. It makes us fools. And it leaves us unwilling to risk, and therefore unwilling to gain the whole world in Jesus.

I am convinced that a big part of what is keeping modern Christians from spiritually flourishing is this: our self-identity. Many of us, I think, subscribe to a mentality I see across evangelicalism. It's this: *I am saved by Christ, but I'm broken and unable to help myself.*

I think many believers conceive of themselves in these terms. *Yes, I'm redeemed. Yes, it's glorious that God has saved me. But I can't really make any headway. I'm broken. My life is two steps ahead, two steps back.* Spirituality = New Year's resolutions. You have a peak: "I'm going to grow in faith this year!" followed by a valley: "I stink, I'm inconsistent, and I always will be."

It's true that we're sinners and always will be while on this earth, but I think the emphasis in this thinking is in the wrong place. Many of us read Romans 7, with Paul detailing a desperate state of mind before the law, and we immediately apply it to ourselves as Christians. To the extent that we're thinking about this kind of thing, we read "I do not do what I want, but I do the very thing I hate" (v. 15) and think, *That's me.* We feel enslaved, and indeed, it seems we are: "I see in my members another law waging war against the law of my mind and making me captive to the law of sin that dwells in my members" (v. 23). There you go.

Now we're not only struggling, but we feel justified in doing so.

Scholars differ in their interpretation of Romans 7. It's a tricky chapter. I think Paul was speaking of captivity to sin *before* his salvation. He had wanted to do what was right, but he realized—now, from the eyes of faith—that without Christ, he couldn't. He had *thought* he could honor God as he knew he should, but he was really enslaved.

If this is true, and I'm right, then the "I'm broken and I can't get up" mentality has taken a major hit. This is huge. Because the way we think about ourselves determines the way we live. This is a point I know personally, and I'm guessing you do too.

I remember a basketball coach taking me aside in my freshman year of high school. I was at a summer camp and struggling with my confidence. Some days I was up; others I was down. This coach, revered in our little Maine community, told me I could be a starter. He said he saw real talent in me. This was the first time a coach had ever said that to me. From then on, I thought of myself differently. I believed I could actually succeed as a basketball player.

I saw myself as a basketball player, not just a kid who loved the game. And that has stayed with me ever since.

You need not have a similar athletic experience to relate to this truth. Maybe you had a piano teacher look you in the eye and encourage you. Or perhaps you had a writing instructor assure you that you wrote well. Maybe you had a drama coach remark that you'd grasped a particular scene in just the right way. Perhaps a grandparent complimented your woodworking, or your freshly baked cookies, and that opened your eyes to see that God had gifted you in certain ways. Encouragement is real, and it often leads us to see how we can serve the Lord in important ways.

Sometimes a whole life's work takes shape around a single comment that helps us unlock who we are and what we are made to do. You find this theme in popular culture. Take the largely unknown film *Dear Frankie*, a 2004 movie that tells the deeply touching story of a boy named Frankie whose mother left her abusive husband. Desperate to give her son a manly role model, she hires a seaman she doesn't know to pretend to be Frankie's father. Frankie is a sad boy; life is hard for him. His is a heartbreaking childhood. But something changes when this man enters his life. He realizes that he is loved. He has a new identity. He gains confidence, meaning, and hope. The transformation is nothing short of stunning.[2]

There's a version of this kind of message that is cheesy. It's based around secular self-esteem and selfish dreams: "I can be whoever I want to be, and I deserve better than what I have." You could call this way of thinking *narcissistic optimistic deism*. It says, "I'm the center of all things," "My life will always get better, because I deserve it," and "I believe in God! He's the granter of all my wishes" (as opposed to his being the *righteous ruler of all things*). God is like the boyfriend in a Bruno Mars or Lady Gaga song, or a hanger-on in a C-list reality-TV star's entourage: he never asks us to change, but exists only to flatter us, build us up, soothe us when something doesn't go the way we want.

That's how many people today approach God: *he exists to make me great.* This is an unhealthy view of God, and it's why we need to be careful when talking with people who say they believe in God. I fear that many today believe in God because they see him as the Great Dream-Granter in the Sky, the one who coddles us and gives us everything we want because it's owed to us. *I'm beautiful; I'm smart; I'm gifted. I deserve to have a nice life because I'm a good person. If things don't go right for me, I'm going to throw a fit, because life is about me and my happiness.*

But that's not what I mean when I say we need spiritual encouragement. I'm not commending here a Disney-fied Christianity borne by selfish dreams. I'm talking about something far greater and incredibly different: you and me existing to make *God* great, discovering our worth and identity in him, not the world and its opinions.

YOU ARE A NEW CREATION

The Lord wishes to give us a new self-understanding grounded in the cross of Christ, which Matthew unfolds at the apex of his gospel:

> Now from the sixth hour there was darkness over all the land until the ninth hour. And about the ninth hour Jesus cried out with a loud voice, saying, "Eli, Eli, lema sabachthani?" that is, "My God, my God, why have you forsaken me?" And some of the bystanders, hearing it, said, "This man is calling Elijah." And one of them at once ran and took a sponge, filled it with sour wine, and put it on a reed and gave it to him to drink. But the others said, "Wait, let us see whether Elijah will come to save him." And Jesus cried out again with a loud voice and yielded up his spirit. (Matt. 27:45–50)

Because Jesus "yielded up his spirit," you and I have access to truly world-shaking power. We may wonder how we can strike out and be like the faithful servants of the parable of the talents. We can only do so because God has saved us through Christ, who was a bold and self-sacrificial deliverer of his people. Because Jesus obeyed the Father and gave his life on the cross, "our old self was crucified with him in order that the body of sin might be brought to nothing, so that we would no longer be enslaved to sin" (Rom. 6:6). Do you see this? You and I can honor the Lord through the power of the cross, because our sin—our old self—was crucified at Calvary.

John Owen, a Puritan teacher who wore one of those killer white wigs, summed up this awesome idea in a book title: *The Death of Death in the Death of Christ*. In other words, Jesus defeated sin at the cross. He killed it. Crushed it. Game over. And then, he defeated death. He rose again, as John shows in his gospel:

> But Mary stood weeping outside the tomb, and as she wept she stooped to look into the tomb. And she saw two angels in white, sitting where the body of Jesus had lain, one at the head and one at the feet. They said to her, "Woman, why are you weeping?" She said to them, "They have taken away my Lord, and I do not know where they have laid him." Having said this, she turned around and saw Jesus standing, but she did not know that it was Jesus. Jesus said to her, "Woman, why are you weeping? Whom are you seeking?" Supposing him to be the gardener, she said to him, "Sir, if you have carried him away, tell me where you have laid him, and I will take him away." Jesus said to her, "Mary." She turned and said to him in Aramaic, "Rabboni!" (John 20:11–16)

Jesus triumphed over the grave, much to the shock of his followers. This is not an abstract fact though. It's not a magnet for your refrigerator, a key chain for your pocket. With the defeat of sin at the cross, the defeat of death through the resurrection means that now we can live righteous lives.

This is a bonfire in your heart.

The gospel message of Jesus' saving work offers us the power to risk everything for him, and gain everything in him. When we come to Jesus, we are not merely punched through to the afterlife though. We are redeemed—all of us. Heart, soul, and mind. The old has passed away. The new has come. This is precisely what Paul tells us: "From now on, therefore, we regard no one according to the flesh. Even though we once regarded Christ according to the flesh, we regard him thus no longer. Therefore, if anyone is in Christ, he is a new creation. The old has passed away; behold, the new has come. All this is from God, who through Christ reconciled us to himself and gave us the ministry of reconciliation" (2 Cor. 5:16–18).

This passage is foundational for bold spirituality. If you're going to pursue the Lord with zeal each day, you need to know the core DNA of your faith. Here it is. Bullet, meet powder. You are not a miserable wretch. You are not 50 percent saved/50 percent wicked. You are in Christ, and you are a "new creation." The old is gone. The new is here.

This isn't your work or mine. God has done this through Christ. On the cross, Jesus bore our sin; through the cross, we gained his righteous standing. This is what his reconciliation means for us. We're no longer outcasts. We're reconciled to God. This is our *fundamental* identity.

God loves us. We are his.

So what does this mean in practical terms? Surely we're saved, but sin is like a bully, right? We try to fight it, but it dominates us? Nope.

Here's Paul again: "We know that our old self was crucified with him in order that the body of sin might be brought to nothing, so that we would no longer be enslaved to sin. For one who has died has been set free from sin" (Rom. 6:6–7).

This word from Paul is for you and me. It's pure relief. We're *not* slaves to sin. It doesn't have power over us. We have been "set free" from it. I simply can't conceive of any more encouraging words than this for a believer.

Sadly, I think many of us have missed this incredible encouragement in our Bibles, or at the very least underplayed it. We believe we have the opposite identity as believers. We think we very much *are* enslaved. Or at least we feel that way. We're defeated. We're not leaving the faith, we're not going out the door, but our heads are on the table, and we're discouraged. Worse, we don't know how to change this sad situation.

Here's how: embrace your identity in Jesus Christ. You are no longer a slave to sin. You are a slave to righteousness. This is a theology of hope. This is gospel spirituality. It's grounded in what God has done in Christ to save and renew sinners. If you will embrace this biblical testimony, you will see growth in your spiritual life.

I recently read about a man under the care of pastor Eugene Peterson. He was a truck driver who was saved at an early age. Over the years, he wandered from the faith. He started going to a Maryland church but wasn't really serious about it. One day he was driving across the country, listening to his CB radio. The talk was disgusting, thoroughly sexual, and something in him snapped. He was used to it, but all of a sudden, he couldn't handle it anymore.

As soon as he got home, he called his pastor and asked him to help him live for the Lord. He got serious about church and became a deacon. As recounted in Peterson's *The Pastor*, he experienced the power of the gospel.

This is the kind of story the Holy Spirit loves to author. It's also the kind that you and I can live out if we will embrace God's renewing grace and let it flood all the channels of our lives.

It's not sin that is unstoppable—it's grace.

YOU ARE MORE THAN A CONQUEROR

If you have read this far, I know that you *do* very much want to grow. Let's close this loop with one more concept from Scripture. You are not only a new creation. You're not only freed from sin. You're a conqueror through Christ. After noting that believers face "tribulation, . . . distress, . . . persecution, . . . famine, . . . nakedness, . . . danger, . . . [and] sword," Paul tells us who we really are in one of the Bible's most soaring passages: "In all these things we are more than conquerors through him who loved us. For I am sure that neither death nor life, nor angels nor rulers, nor things present nor things to come, nor powers, nor height nor depth, nor anything else in all creation, will be able to separate us from the love of God in Christ Jesus our Lord" (Rom. 8:35, 37–39).

Many people profess to offer hope as Christian pastors and leaders. But sometimes when you get right down to their reasoning, it's not really grounded in much—some airy promises about

God wanting to unconditionally bless us, followed by a celebration of our world-shaking awesomeness.

The Bible offers us tremendous hope, but note where it's grounded: in the wisdom and kindness of almighty God. He doesn't owe his people anything. But as the apostle makes clear, God has freely chosen to "graciously give us all things" in Jesus (Rom. 8:32). He has justified us such that we are no longer condemned in God's sight. We are by nature criminals before a holy God, but through the cross he has granted us righteous standing in his divine courtroom. Jesus is now interceding for us, and nothing can stop him from doing so. Nothing can separate us from his love. For us and all the redeemed from all of history, this love is unstoppable. It can't be disarmed, overpowered, canceled, or refused.

What does all of this mean? What does it boil down to? Whatever our earthly circumstances, we are "more than conquerors" in Christ (Rom. 8:37). It's as if the world is a battlefield and we're walking around just after the battle's close. We're triumphant. Our enemy is vanquished. The powers of darkness are defeated.

That is how every Christian can and should live. We see the smoke rising from a great spiritual conflict, but it's not telling us we've lost. It's a sign of Christ's victory over sin, death, and Satan. That victory is ours. That's the reality in which we live, every single day, no matter what we're facing.

This doesn't mean, though, that all of life is smooth sailing. We are still tempted by our old nature (Col. 3:1–11). We have to "put it off" and kill it. Sin is defeated but not eliminated. That happens either when we die and go to heaven or when Christ returns and we reign with him (1 Thess. 4:16–17). But while we live here, in this in-between age, you could put it like this: Once, we were sin addicts. Now the power of addiction has been broken. But just like a former alcoholic or drug addict, we will have to continually choose not to give in to our old temptations. They don't have power over us; they can't control us. They're defeated. But they're not eradicated, and so each day we must choose not to allow sin and its fruits to master us.

I was recently reminded of the power of the gospel in renewing us when I came across the story of a woman named Holly. She had two abortions early in life and was convicted about this terrible sin. But in her words, she "chose to be blind" to it, even after joining a church.

Here's what she shared about her journey to repentance:

> I was able to live for a number of years as if the two babies I'd killed weren't that big a deal, as if they never existed. But, whenever the topic of abortion came up in any circumstance, especially at church, I was overwhelmed with feelings of shame, condemnation, and guilt. My voluntary blindness didn't serve me in those moments. I was trying to keep this piece of my life hidden in the dark.
>
> But the Lord had other plans, and he called me to bring what was sin into the light . . . It wasn't until I saw my sin for what it was, saw it for how brutal and awful it was, saw it for how the Lord sees it—only then could I truly come to repentance and recognize that I needed my Savior . . . I was reminded that Jesus died for me and gave me his righteousness before the Father (my new identity!), I could see the incredible magnificence of his lavish grace poured out on me, a sinner.

As the Lord drew Holly near, he broke her addiction to sin. She realized that repentance was not a burden, but a means of liberation, the only true liberation there is. She saw by God's grace that she was not in chains to sin, but could be free.

Holly repented and conquered her sin through Christ. Now she's a deaconess at a thriving church in one of America's darkest cities. The Lord is using her to counsel women just like her, and lead them to victory in Jesus.

That's what God loves to do, and that's what he *will* do in our lives.

HOW TO TRANSCEND THE SUFFERING THAT WILL COME

Being "more than a conqueror" means that we have overcome the world, but we will continue to live in a fallen realm and feel its sting. This is what Jesus explicitly stated in John 16:33: "In the world you will have tribulation. But take heart; I have overcome the world." We will have "tribulation," which means pain, hardship, suffering. I don't know what you were promised when you became a believer, but this is Jesus' promise to us. So when we experience tough stuff in this world, we must not think that we were offered a different package.

If you're going to live with Christ, you're going to suffer with him.

That has profound importance for our spirituality. It means that we shouldn't flail and thrash when the kids are sick, it's hard to pray, or we find it challenging to actually get into the Word. These and other struggles are not signs that you're *not* a

Christian; they may very well be signs that you *are*. Think about Job, who lost everything, not in spite of his faith, but *because* of it (see Job 1). Not everyone will know such dramatic trial, but we will all taste pain in some way. Being a follower of Christ enters you into a spiritual battle. It doesn't take you out of it. It may not always feel like it, but this is right where you're supposed to be. In God's providence, the "tribulation" we all face in some way is a means of grace. It's intended to grow our faith and give glory to God.

Let me tell you about one example of this from my life. I met Ralph Knowles in my college years. He lived in an aging home, he had retired from the flower business, and he wasn't known by the wider world. When my friends and I met him, he was recovering from the death of his wife, whom he had adored. Every time he would talk about her, then and later, his eyes would tear up.

Mr. Knowles knew the pain and struggle that grow like weeds in a fallen world. But that was not his story. He made a deep impression on my friends and me because he lived every minute for the glory of God. He redeemed his retirement by writing evangelistic letters to prison inmates, cooking food for needy church members, and generally lighting up his entire block with his smile and zest for life. Mr. Knowles wasn't a world-trotting missionary. He was an eighty-year-old man living in a small town in Maine.

But make no mistake—he was on mission for Christ. He was living life to the full.

Over the years, with much practice, Mr. Knowles built a godly walk with Christ. He did it through the sheer mercy and grace of God. He was more than a conqueror.

You and I are just like him. We, too, are "more than conquerors." The Spirit resides in us, enabling us to know God as Father and lose ourselves in his love (Rom. 8:8–16). The Spirit is the "Helper" sent by Jesus into the heart of every post-Pentecost believer (John 16:7). We don't have to sign a form or pass a spiritual fitness test for him to occupy our hearts. Jesus has given him to us, and he guides us "into all the truth" (John 16:13). The Spirit is such a transformative presence in the believer's life that Christ makes the momentous statement that it's better for his disciples to have the Spirit than to be in Christ's presence (John 16:7).

The Helper, praise God, has come.

GOOD NEWS FOR DISCOURAGED CHRISTIANS

All of the preceding boils down to this: we have a great task before us, but we have even greater power working in us. Our central encouragement is this: God doesn't leave us alone. He calls us to a great mission, offers us tremendous adventure, but then surprises us by telling us that he will be right beside us. He's always worked this way. As he said before he executed the exodus from Egypt, the watershed event of the Old Testament and a preview of Christ's deliverance of his people, "I will take you to be my people, and I will be your God, and you shall know that I am the LORD your God, who has brought you out from under the burdens of the Egyptians" (Ex. 6:7).

God repeated this promise in the New Testament to his disciples just after he charged them with the evangelizing of the entire world. Like the Exodus, the Great Commission was no small task—and this was no small guarantee:

> Now the eleven disciples went to Galilee, to the mountain to which Jesus had directed them. And when they saw him they worshiped him, but some doubted. And Jesus came and said to them, "All authority in heaven and on earth has been given to me. Go therefore and make disciples of all nations, baptizing them in the name of the Father and of the Son and of the Holy Spirit, teaching them to observe all that I have commanded you. And behold, I am with you always, to the end of the age." (Matt. 28:16–20)

This is a declaration of utter solidarity. It is a means of infinite strength. To be with God, to have him with us, is to be in the presence of pure joy, no matter what we're facing.

One way of talking about our relationship with the Lord is to say that we have "union" with God, just as a married couple is in union. Because of the Spirit residing in us, we can truly say that we are "in Christ" and he is "in [us]" (2 Cor. 5:17; 1 Cor. 3:16). The Holy Spirit is not simply *out there*, but is inside all who have repented of their sin and placed their faith in Christ.

This is true in my experience—wonderfully so. I'm a sinner. I don't do everything I should. But I can look back at my life— even as a young man—and see that God has done good work in me. He has upgraded my faith over the years. He's enabled me to kill sin and to build habits of godliness such that I'm not having to start from square one every day. This is what God wants to do with us: to train us in holiness, build us up, and leave us changed and changing.

Does this mean I never falter? That all my bad habits are gone? Well, no. As I write this, I'm gearing up to apologize to my wife for forgetting to follow through on a task. Let's put it this way: my sins and weaknesses definitely have been used to increase my sweet wife's patience over the years! Despite my failures, though, the Lord has done good work in me.

He will continue to do that for me, and for you.

Remember, after all, that we're not called to glorify the Lord by our own efforts, but through the Spirit's power. This is exactly what Paul tells us in Romans 8:10–11: "But if Christ is in you, although the body is dead because of sin, the Spirit is life because of righteousness. If the Spirit of him who raised Jesus from the dead dwells in you, he who raised Christ Jesus from the dead will also give life to your mortal bodies through his Spirit who dwells in you." The same Spirit who raised Jesus from the dead has raised you and me from the dead. This is, we could say, the gospel come alive in our hearts and minds.

What a sweet comfort for all of us—the undisciplined, the unkind, the anxious, the jealous, the greedy, the selfish, the sinner.

Here's a term by which to think about your identity as a Christian: *empowered dependence*. You and I are empowered by the Spirit, as we've discussed. But though spiritually alive, we're not autonomous. In other words, we don't get saved and then set out on our own. For the rest of our lives, we walk beside the Lord, who leads us, as Psalm 23 so poignantly teaches.

We're not responsible for our spiritual vitality. All of that comes from God, from what is called our "union" with Christ, given us by the indwelling Spirit.

Consider the iPad. It's a powerful little machine, capable of doing tons of stuff (including, for many, such essential tasks as the killing of angry virtual birds). But it has no power without its source, without a charge. We're like the iPad. God empowers us. He frees us up to serve him in a million ways, but never without his power.

So we live out lives of *empowered dependence*, gaining strength and victory through God in us. We're not weak or defeated, but neither are we autonomous or independent. We do sin, sadly, but the Spirit never fails us, never lets us down, never falters in answering our spiritual need. He is always present with us, and his ministry is one of continual empowerment (John 14:14–17). Take away the Spirit, and we're left to our own devices. We will surely flounder and fall flat. Give us the Spirit, as God does to everyone he saves, and we are "more than conquerors" in any and all situations (Rom. 8:37). That, my friends, is transformative truth.

That is a theology of hope.

CONCLUSION

Christopher Duffley was born, if you recall, weighing barely more than a pound. His body was ravaged by the effects of drugs that passed through his system in the womb. He was destitute and without hope in the world. But he was adopted by Christian parents. He was loved. He was nurtured. And he has become something greater than his circumstances dictated. It was the love of his family—the knowledge of his acceptance—that made his transformation possible.[3]

So it will be for us, if we open our eyes to who we are in Christ. This is how you can be a person of bold faith. You've heard the call from chapter 2; here in chapter 3, you've seen how the gospel supplies the power you need to answer that call.

Now, my friends, it's time to turn conviction into action.

INTERMISSION: RISKING TO BUILD

Let me pause and ask you a question: When was the last time you built something big?

Or how about this: When did you last do something challenging and hard that seemed impossible, but then, when you were finished, yielded immense satisfaction?

If you're like me, there may not be an avalanche of experience from which to draw, at least in the building department. I'm happy if I can "build" (stretching the word here) a basic dresser for my little girl. I have, though, done some hard things in my life, and they have given me much satisfaction. You know the type of accomplishments: running many miles, learning a new trade or skill, earning a degree, restoring a car, and so on.

These projects are great. When was the last time, though, that we invested in our spiritual lives with this same kind of attitude?

Christianity isn't foremost about fun or adventure or extreme sports. It's about following Christ, which may mean hardship and even death. But here's what I'm after: I think we're missing something if we don't embark on this journey with our Savior with a sense of grand destiny.

This kind of vision, as we talked about in chapter 1, is uncommon today. A feeling of courageous adventure seems absent from our faith. I wonder if we've lost something that Abraham and David and Paul might have tasted.

If that's true, that's not good. Here's some encouragement: if we've lost it, we can get it back.

We've introduced this theme through what I've called "gospel risk," which means trading in small things that produce a shallow, defeated life for the life shaped by the gospel, one devoted to God and his glory. We "risk" the world and gain everything in Christ. Now that we've covered this concept, I want to introduce a second core idea: building stuff. I mean, specifically, investing in God-honoring pursuits, like our spiritual lives, families, churches, and jobs.

The parable of the talents covered in chapter 2 commended just this kind of spirit. The faithful servants created more. Out of a sense of greater purpose and mission, they "built" greater wealth. You can apply this mind-set to a whole range of areas. This "make more" perspective is uniquely helpful as an approach to the Christian life. Of course, God is the ultimate Builder and Creator. He's the One who makes humankind in his image and commissions them to "have dominion" over the earth (Gen. 1:26–27). I don't think we've thought enough about this crucial reality. I certainly don't think many of us have consciously applied it to all areas of our lives.

Too often, we think that godliness means careening around without any real direction, shooting off like a space shuttle with a deficient navigating system. Our lives follow whatever paths the Lord desires, but let's remember that godliness is closely related to routine, commitment, hard work, and tireless pursuit. The Bible, as we will see, teaches us to invest our lives in certain core institutions and areas. Many of us have missed this; we will profit from recovering this idea.

Taking dominion means more than naming animals and tending plants, as in the earliest days of Adam. The concept extends beyond the earth's formation to our own age. By subduing our sins, creating families as we can (earthly and spiritual), growing in discipline, working as image-bearers, and constructing godly lives, we take dominion.

We build.

Remember Matthew 7:24–25 as you move ahead. Toward the close of his Sermon on the Mount, the most famous sermon ever preached, Jesus said this: "Everyone then who hears these words of mine and does them will be like a wise man who built his house on the rock. And the rain fell, and the floods came, and the winds blew and beat on that house, but it did not fall, because it had been founded on the rock."

God wants us to risk, to exchange a small, fearful life for a bold, confident one, and all because of the fact that Jesus will sustain us and bless us as we do so. From this foundation, through the Spirit's power, we are free to be gospel builders, to create a life of faith and action. It is worthwhile. It will be adventurous; it will be momentous. After all, we have a cause that is infinitely more exciting than the fun but temporary pursuits of those around us. We get to live for Christ's magnification, which makes all worldly adventures and hobbies and accomplishments—however fun—pale in comparison.

Now, through prayer and an awareness of our empowered dependence, it's time to get to work.

4 RISKY SPIRITUALITY: BUILDING A STRONGER FAITH

He's wild, you know. Not like a tame lion.

—C. S. Lewis on Aslan in *The Lion,*
the Witch, and the Wardrobe

DID YOU EVER HEAR ABOUT THE "GOOF ON THE ROOF"? Get ready to file this one under "Things You Can't Make Up."

His name was Ronald Stach. He was a die-hard Baltimore Ravens fan who took his team so seriously that he resolved to live on the roof of a city bar until the team won a game (this was before the team began winning Super Bowls). The stunt attracted local and then national attention. It also drew the ire of Stach's estranged wife, who made clear that she would rather he pay his child support than devote himself to a sports team.[1]

Yes, you read that right. Stach's devotion to his team eclipsed his devotion to his family (and more than forty thousand dollars in support). The factoid first makes us laugh (the nickname is funny) and then, after we investigate a little bit, makes us upset at the suffering this man's wife and child faced.

But it draws a third reaction, the more we think about it. There's a parable here for us, a lesson. The Goof on the Roof sums up one of the chief temptations we face as creatures of a modern age: to take serious things unseriously, and unserious things seriously. We are not that different from Ronald Stach. We, too, are inclined to opt out of what truly matters, and to buy into what is quickly fading. We need grace just like he does.

We need to be changed.

In the previous chapter, we discussed the biblical foundation for a life of bold faith. Chapter 2 showed that all Christians are called to live boldly for God. Chapter 3 presented the ways God empowers us to answer this call. The gospel, we saw, is the foundation of Christian growth. There is no lasting change, no true transformation, without the sin-killing, death-defeating power of God in us.

In this chapter, we're going to build off of that foundation. We're going to make the life of bold faith intensely practical. Our goal here is to apply the power of the gospel to every area of our lives. This happens by (1) knowing that we are more than conquerors and (2) actually conquering our flesh and replacing it with virtue. Holiness does not boil down to *either* grace or effort. It's grounded in God's grace, but it happens as we, through the Spirit's agency, practically "put off" sin and "put on" godliness (see Col. 3:1–11).

Let's look into how this practical growth can happen. In the pages that follow, we're going to consider several practices that will allow us to grow in holiness.

THE ALL-CONSUMING PROBLEM OF DISCIPLINE

I remember the first time I tried to be disciplined in prayer. Maybe you had a similar experience. I saw that I needed to devote myself to prayer, so I set out to pray for half an hour. Target: set. Locked and loaded, I launched in.

I prayed up a storm. Everything I could think of. The wind howled; the earth shook. Moses and the saints interrupted their heavenly discussions to peer down through filmy clouds at this fledgling mystic. This was *serious* prayer.

As I wound to a close, I let my words trail off. A prayer warrior had been forged. A lifetime of supplication had begun. I looked at the clock with a sense of pietistic triumph . . .

. . . and saw that exactly nine minutes had elapsed. And—*wince*—my knees hurt from kneeling.

I realized, at that point, that there was more to being fervent in prayer than just setting goals and having good intentions. I would need to be disciplined, and most important, to grow in holiness so I'd actually, you know, have things to *pray for*. This would take time, I realized; I had no trouble watching movies or playing a video game for hours on end. But my discipline did not extend to my spiritual life.

I hadn't cultivated a serious relationship with the Lord to that point. I needed God to move in me to give me a greater hunger and thirst for righteousness (see Matt. 5:6, a great verse on which to meditate). I also needed to grow in discipline so I could actually draw near to the Lord.

Looking back, my example is humorous. But I think it captures where many of us find ourselves and where our culture is today. We have good intentions, but we lack discipline. This can take many forms:

- We don't want to suffer.
- We struggle with sweat.
- We'd rather go under a surgical knife than amend our eating habits.
- We hear a call to action, and we translate it into legalism.
- We don't want to stop engaging media that we shouldn't.
- We have a hard time doing the vocational stuff that we don't like.
- We can't be bothered to commit to a church.

Of course, we *say* we want to change. But what happens when someone actually calls us on a sin or suggests some way to grow? Often, our self-justification instincts kick in. We give lots of reasons and excuses for our behavior. We pretend to like discipline, but in reality, we like it on paper. We sometimes struggle to enact it.

Maybe it even offends us when someone suggests that we do.

It's easy to be theoretically disciplined. Think about the gym. You make your resolution. You buy the stretchy pants, get the killer water bottle, and you're good to go. You print off the workout plan, meet your workout partner, and you're ready to climb the Mountaintop of Health. But then things gets busy, your arms ache so much you can barely raise them to open the door, and when the alarm rings, you convince yourself that what your body needs most is not more exercise—banish the thought! —but rest.

Have you been there? I've been there. We all have. Theoretical discipline is easy; consistent, committed discipline is a bit harder. Such is the human condition.

But I wonder if, in the end, this is really true. Is the problem actually that we're not disciplined? If we're honest, I think the answer is no.

What do I mean? Most of us are in fact able to apply our passions to certain pursuits. We can reach our goals. But here's the deal: we're not naturally, in our sin, inclined to embrace godly discipline. It goes the other way. We've been trained by our fallen natures to pursue and work for things that don't truly satisfy.

We don't lack discipline, you see. We lack discipline in the right *direction*.

Think about this on a practical level. When it comes to our appetite for fun and entertainment, we are not merely disciplined. Our quest to make ourselves happy in the ways we like approaches levels of devotion associated with ultramarathons or hunger fasts. We have discipline, all right: discipline for hedonism, self-satisfaction, pleasure.

Call it *self-driven discipline*.

Our favorite TV shows? You couldn't make us miss that must-watch reality program on fashion if you stole all five of the remotes it takes to DVR them. Our fantasy football league? We conduct more research on who to draft in round seven than paralegals working on billion-dollar settlements. Going to sports events or concerts of the artists we love? *Of course* we can postpone our studying or call in sick for work. You only live once, right? Buying the latest offerings from the technology gods? We'll wear the same clothes for a month if it means we can access the cloud whenever we want. Getting the coffee and treats we want? You couldn't stop us from that Starbucks run if you personally took hold of the wind, the rain, and the snow. Nothing keeps us from our $4.50 coffee—truly nothing.

You know what these patterns show us? You and I are serious about what we want to be serious about.

REORIENTING OUR PERSPECTIVE
AROUND WHAT MATTERS

It's no bad thing to enjoy God's good gifts in the world; in fact, it's a good thing! But what these humorous questions show us, I think, is that we really are disciplined. Whether you run your life with military precision or prefer to shuffle around in socks and a T-shirt, we're all willing to sacrifice for what we love. Self-driven discipline is not a rarity; it's a given for us.

I see this in my own life. I don't naturally have a problem getting excited about watching a movie I've been wanting to see. Nobody has to talk me into going to see the latest Christopher Nolan film. Maybe it's different for you—maybe you think Nolan's epic films are boring. Your thing may be totally different—clothes or team sports or rock climbing or friends or high fashion or celebrity culture or comic books or Greek philosophy. Passions will vary. But you understand my point. When it comes to me plugging into things that truly matter, that's where the tension pops up. It's when I come home after a long day and need to show love to my sweet and hyper kids that I feel the tension.

I remember a heartbreaking song called "Underneath the Door" by the musician Michael Card about how his father, a doctor, would shut himself up in his study after an exhausting day at work. As a little boy, desperate to interact with his dad, Michael would slide pictures under the door. He wanted nothing more than to sit with his father, wrestle with him, *be loved by him*. I hear that story and I feel little Michael's pain. I've always sided with him as I've turned his narrative over in my mind.

But now that I'm the father of two little kids, I see the other side. As with all our sin, self-justification for this selfish behavior comes naturally. I tell myself, *Yeah, I'm not being Dad of the Year right now, but I'm tired. Can't I just get a few minutes to myself?* Do you see what self-driven discipline does? It talks us out of self-giving. The fundamental call of Christ is to take up our crosses and follow him, but our selfish nature doesn't want us to sacrifice. Satan wants us to pity ourselves, turn away from self-sacrifice, and justify our selfishness with a thousand excuses.

You know what this all means? It means that when I am selfish, I am not living according to the biblical idea of gospel risk. I'm embracing comfort and ease and selfishness. I'm turning down the opportunity given me by the Spirit to be like Christ. The opportunity to "make more talents" (see chapter 2) and grow in godliness and love is right there before me. All the blessings of obedience and holiness are before my eyes. My children, furthermore, wait to reward my attention with their adorable enthusiasm.

You could think of our selfish pursuits in this way: they are false gospels. They offer us satisfaction. They promise us lasting fulfillment: "If I can just have X, then I'll be truly happy." If we could just have exactly what we want right now, then all the hardships of life would melt away and we could be joyfully content. We live our lives in this pattern, training ourselves to find fulfillment and happiness in things that have one—and only one—trait in common: they are not God.

They are not the gospel.

What does this mean practically? It means we discipline ourselves to pursue things that aren't worth the effort. We're chasing a false gospel of satisfaction, whether it's looking a certain way, having the right friends, getting the optimal job, being free of familiar struggles, making a certain amount of money, having a lot of free time, getting to travel and eat and exercise, or many other pursuits. We zealously pursue these promises of fulfillment, thinking they will relieve our longings.

But they won't.

GETTING A PLAN

Let's be clear: it's not wrong to like food and iPhones and singer-songwriters. It's no bad thing for busy men and women to get a moment to themselves. Many of the fun things I've mentioned to this point are good gifts of God and can be used in appropriate ways. I actually think God intends for us to enjoy the common things of this world.

But here's the thing: nothing in this world will satisfy us outside of Jesus Christ. It's not stuff or a state of mind that you and I should crave; it's Christ. It's entirely right to want to enjoy life, and it's good to seek the relief of personal suffering. But achieving a goal, any goal, or getting what we want, any want, is not going to satisfy us in an ultimate sense.

That is a false gospel.

What we need instead is more of God. More of Christ. More of the true gospel, which is grounded in the tenacious commitment of a Messiah to the eternal salvation of his people.

We need, in short, to be holier, devoted to the Lord, and satisfied by him. That is the central need of our lives. That is the cause worth every sacrifice. Jesus Christ, and nothing else, is the One whose grandeur and love and power deserve the zealous discipline of our minds, hearts, and souls.

But holiness doesn't just happen. That's true even if you love the gospel. Piety—the practice of godliness—does not equal *thinking* about spiritual truths. It means knowing truth, and then putting those truths into *action*. You can only do that if you are disciplined. And you can only be disciplined if you have a plan.

That's the way, in other words, that we overcome self-driven discipline, the natural inclination of our hearts to pursue small things as though we are great and they will fulfill us. We aren't great; they won't fulfill us.

We do, however, find the kind of life our hearts crave when we risk worldly things and pursue *gospel-driven discipline*.

As we saw in the previous chapter, God saves us to unleash us. We once were unable to please him. But now, because of the work of Christ, we are new people, new creations. We are not miserable worms unable to do anything at all to honor God. As Christians, we are in Christ, and totally new. We are called now to savor the gospel and then move to action. We must do what 1 Timothy 4:7 calls for: "Discipline yourself for the purpose of godliness" (NASB), a call that requires exactly what it says—discipline. Effort. Hard work. The formation of good habits, and the unlearning of bad ones. This kind of Christianity isn't legalistic and works-based and harmful to happiness. It's how we taste God's goodness.

Read 1 Peter 1:13–16 with me: "Therefore, preparing your minds for action, and being sober-minded, set your hope fully on the grace that will be brought to you at the revelation of Jesus Christ. As obedient children, do not be conformed to the passions of your former ignorance, but as he who called you is holy, you also be holy in all your conduct, since it is written, 'You shall be holy, for I am holy.'"

The root of holiness is "the grace" found in Jesus. Grace is not dormant, however; it is not fuzzy. It has shape and form. It has edges. Those who have been captured by grace calibrate their "minds for action," pursuing holiness in everything they do. They see that holiness is not optional. Neither does it happen without effort. There is no daily holiness drink that we consume like spiritual Powerade. We don't get zapped each morning by a righteousness lightning bolt. Contrary to some evangelical thinking, we have to put in effort to grow in godliness.

Maybe you're thinking, *That's all well and good, but, um, I'm not very disciplined at being disciplined in holiness.*

If this is true of you—and I think it's true of all of us if we're honest—we have tremendously good news in Scripture. We have endless hope and power in God. If we find ourselves struggling in the small things, we find encouragement in the biblical truth that God never fails his people. Of course, we're not perfect now, and we won't be until we are glorified. We're living in the tension of being already saved but not yet made perfect. This means that even as we achieve victory over sin, we'll frankly still continue to sin. We'll disappoint ourselves. We'll let other people down. We'll dishonor God. This isn't defeatism. It's just the truth.

But remember this as we move ahead: there's never a moment when we earnestly go to the Lord for spiritual power and he denies us. Wherever you are right now, here's the good news: there is no limit to God's goodness. We never withdraw an installment of grace only to see the screen blinking angrily at us, "ACCOUNT OVERDRAWN! ACCOUNT OVERDRAWN!" The kindness of the Lord never runs dry. The mercy of God never stops.

So grace is the fuel to holiness. Peter says it so well: "His divine power has granted to us all things that pertain to life and godliness" (2 Peter 1:3). That's it right there. Everything we need to grow in grace *is here*, as we covered at length in chapter 3. This is the irreplaceable and absolutely necessary foundation of gospel-driven discipline. Without it, everything else fails.

Here's what we're going to do now: map out a strategy by which to reach our spiritual potential. We do not want to be those who waste their gifts. We want to be like those who take what God has given them and become something greater.

STEPS TO BOLD SPIRITUALITY

With the previous section firmly and necessarily fixed in our minds, let's consider some practical steps we can take to worship the Lord in our daily lives. These habits will enable us to begin building a strong walk of faith with Christ.

Establish daily rhythms. One of the best things you can do for your spiritual life is this: get your daily life in order.

If you're struggling to kill sin and be disciplined, as so many of us are, you should make it a matter of first priority to structure your life. Go to bed at a certain time; get a lot of sleep; rise early; start studying or get to work at a good hour; work steadily through the day. Eat good meals at sensible hours, and standardize them as much as you can. Get regular exercise, whether that's walking, running, sports, or other means. If you impose discipline on your body, I guarantee you'll be better equipped to impose it on your soul.

This is especially important for you if you're a young person. Modern college and postcollege life can easily take on unprofitable shape if we're not careful.

I remember reading a story about baseball commissioner Bud Selig. He ate the same breakfast every single day—eggs and toast, I believe. He went to the same homespun restaurant, got his coffee, read his newspaper, and ate his eggs and toast. Without fail, with no variation or shadow due to change. (I've done something similar. At one point in my life, I had a Sunbelt chocolate chip granola bar every day for six years straight. I'm still kind of proud of that, actually.)

Are we talking about spiritual eggs and toast though—does a disciplined life mean being endlessly rote and regimented? It can, I suppose. But here's my prediction: you will get a great deal more out of life if you avoid an anti-schedule, fun-obsessed approach to your day. As a young person, you'll have all kinds of opportunities to have fun, and that's great. But don't buy the myth that adulthood is about rejecting rules and discipline. It's about learning to embrace structure so you will experience God's goodness in the midst of responsibility. That's what adulthood is, after all: being stable and steadfast in the face of a host of challenges, including the occasional dullness of life that we all experience.

Whatever your current stage in life, target these things:

1. Establish regular sleep habits.
2. Observe a healthy, balanced diet.
3. Get regular exercise.
4. Turn down some events and activities to be structured.
5. Organize your work hours to be efficient. Break up tasks.
6. Carve out time to rest, relax, and recharge.

This is just a starting point, and it holds throughout life. The connection between your body and your heart is surprising but inescapable. Remember Proverbs 25:28, which says, "A man without self-control is like a city broken into and left without walls." Self-control in every area matters. If you train your body to be disciplined, you will have a far easier time training your heart to be disciplined.

Have a regular (daily) time of prayer and Bible reading. If you want to know the Lord, you simply must set aside time to get to know him through his Word. There's nothing magical here. The Bible is not going to hover overhead each morning and download itself into your brain. Sorry—there's no app for that!

So, set a goal for your study. Maybe it's fifteen minutes of reading, fifteen minutes of prayer to start. Use a Bible reading plan, or just read through the Scripture. If you don't want a formal plan, read two chapters from the Old Testament and one from the New Testament each day. Or find a format that you like. Think about studying a good commentary alongside your reading. Pray out of the overflow of your reading. Pray throughout the day if you can, not merely in your devotional time. Offer different kinds of prayers to God each day: thanksgiving, adoration, confession, requests. Pray in direct response to events in your day. Don't compartmentalize prayer, but constantly lift up your voice to God.

Having this regular (ideally daily) time will set you on the right foot each day, especially if you can do this in the morning. It will set you up to feel what you know—that you are more than a conqueror.

Detox. So you're a sinner, right? Yeah? Me too. Here's the deal: if you're going to kill that sin and grow in godliness per 1 Timothy 4:7–8, you need to get a plan. You do not grow in grace by accident. You grow by effort.

For many of us, this will mean detoxification. Don't be afraid *at all* of stepping away from a pursuit or interest for a time, or even permanently. That won't singlehandedly obliterate sin, but it may very well weaken its hold over a part of your life.

The idea of "detoxing," or removing from our presence the things that tempt us, is not fashionable today. It's much more common for us to bemoan our sins and feel bad about them, but not really do that much to separate ourselves from them. We know we're trapped, and we don't like that. But we can't imagine actually depriving ourselves of things we like.

Think about it. Many young men—and an increasing number of young women—struggle with sexual temptation. Much of this nowadays is connected to the computer. How many guys, though, would be willing to accept radical limits on their computer usage? Or let's say you're a lonely young woman who watches trashy reality-TV shows at night to entertain yourself. Are you willing to shake up your viewing habits for a while to carve some good paths for yourself?

What would you honestly answer to such a question? A good number of us, if we're honest, might say no. We're not willing. When it comes to holiness, it seems, we've lost what you could call the "killer instinct."

The killer instinct is alive and well though, in modern culture. If you're into sports, think of athletes like Kobe Bryant. He nicknamed himself the "Black Mamba," and a few years ago said that he was basketball's best "killer," meaning heroic clutch player, since Michael Jordan. Fans love this kind of player (or they hate him, depending on which team he's on). Though they're not much fun to play with, they win games.

You don't need to know the names of NBA players to see that this instinct has a strong cultural presence. Many of the fashion world's leading lights have made no bones about succeeding due to ruthless will and laser focus. Anna Wintour of *Vogue* magazine is renowned for her icy demeanor and willingness to do whatever is needed to succeed. According to a *60 Minutes* report my wife and I saw, she's got no fewer than three assistants running around at all times, circling her like asteroids around a planet (a very fashionable one, admittedly). What do these examples show us? They reveal that the drive to succeed is very much alive. In fact, it may be more alive in our twenty-first-century culture than ever before.

Except, it sometimes seems, in Christianity.

Where this is true, it doesn't make sense. You could go so far as to say that the spiritual killer instinct originated with Christ. Think freshly about Jesus' words in Matthew 5:27–30:

> You have heard that it was said, "You shall not commit adultery." But I say to you that everyone who looks at a woman

with lustful intent has already committed adultery with her in his heart. If your right eye causes you to sin, tear it out and throw it away. For it is better that you lose one of your members than that your whole body be thrown into hell. And if your right hand causes you to sin, cut it off and throw it away. For it is better that you lose one of your members than that your whole body go into hell.

Jesus didn't intend for his hearers and readers to take these words literally, despite what some early Christians thought. Few of us would have any body parts left if we destroyed those that we used for sin. He did mean, however, that his followers must be utterly ruthless in killing sin.

You think your favorite quarterback is tough? Does your favorite actress wield an iron will? You haven't seen anything yet. The Christian is equipped—and called—to be a far more disciplined person than any politician, business leader, or diva. We are to have a killer instinct, and it has a target: sin.

I'm thankful for Christians who live this kind of life, and I've known many. A close friend of mine didn't grow up watching a bunch of junk on television. She's always had strong faith and a sensitive conscience. When she was young, she went to the home of some friends who put on an inappropriate movie (and whose parents consented). On the spot, she called her father and asked him to pick her up and take her home because she knew that watching this romantic film would tempt her to sin.

She knew her limits, and she acted to stay within them.

This friend of mine continues to make such difficult but God-honoring decisions. She's not motivated by judgmental piety or wide-eyed squeamishness in being careful with film and television programs. She wants to honor the Lord, to keep her heart pure, and to take whatever action is needed to flee from temptation and youthful lusts[2] (2 Tim. 2:22). Sometimes this kind of serious faith comes under fire. Sometimes we make fun of such people. In reality, though, these kinds of hard decisions give great glory to God.

Can you and I act along similar lines? I think we can. Doing so won't make us more saved or likely to be converted at the end of our lives. It will, however, help put our sin to death. You could, for example:

stop going to college parties if they tempt you in various ways

stop watching sports for a while if they suck you into an unserious world

get rid of video games if you play them by the hour and are seeing them wreak havoc on your studying or your relationships

stop hanging out with the opposite sex as "just friends" if you feel your heart tugged

slow down your relationship-building if you're finding the people you're evangelizing are dragging you down spiritually

stop using a computer in class if you can't stop checking Facebook or entertainment sites

refrain from watching movies that encourage you to adopt ungodly behavior

swear off "raunch comedies" if you're drawn to them,
   or "chick flicks" if they draw your heart away from
   contentment

close your account if social media is distracting you from
   Bible study or causing you to be narcissistic (it's okay; I
   promise)

avoid stores or restaurants that bring out your inner
   glutton

Let's be clear: detoxing can't cure us of sin. It's not all we need to do. And it may not be the right strategy for every battle we're fighting. We certainly need the support and accountability of our brothers and sisters. Our churches, after all, are partners with us in our sanctification.

But don't miss the potentially helpful role of detoxing. It is a good thing to approach sin with deadly seriousness. The killer instinct is not a bad thing when it comes to the evil within. It is a serious help.

Set patterns and create habits to foil sin. The crucial ingredient here is discipline. Discipline yourself for the purpose of godliness. Are you tempted to sexual sin when you have free time? Then put your computer in the most public room of your house. Get Covenant Eyes on your computer. Enlist church members and an elder to keep you accountable. In the way that *Every Man's Battle*[3] helpfully discusses, train your eyes not to linger on an attractive figure.

If you use social media, ask your friends to keep you accountable about what you post. Don't post narcissistic updates that ask for attention; you would never do that in conversation, so you probably shouldn't do it online, right? Instead of surfing photos, close the computer, tuck it away, and read an edifying book. If Pinterest (or whatever else) is occupying hours of your time, then either (1) close your account, or (2) institute serious discipline on the site. Put a timer on if you want to visit it.

Do not, my friends, shy away from tough measures when it comes to spirituality. We're not afraid of discipline when it comes to athletic training. We hear about marathoners running 125 miles a week, and we're instantly impressed. We don't look down on actresses or actors or entrepreneurs who work incessantly at their craft. In fact, we praise them for their single-mindedness.

Let me give you an example. I read recently about Steve Jobs, the former CEO of Apple, the company that has conquered the civilized world (and its wallets). Jobs was a major achiever, but according to the recent biography entitled *Steve Jobs* by Walter Isaacson, he was not a very nice man. He wore soft-necked black turtlenecks and looked like a mellow guru, but he drove an incredibly hard pace at Apple. He had little patience for the feelings or situations of those around him, and he did little to mentor and show kindness to his staff. He was, however, an exceptionally driven man, one who was successful at assembling a talented team and then subsequently pushing that team to create amazing products.

Jobs had the ability, in fact, to completely reframe expectations. He might hear a proposal for a product that would reasonably take, say, two years. He would fire questions at the employees giving the presentation, then order them to get the product to market in a matter of months. The flabbergasted team would pull their hair out wondering how they could fit such a demanding schedule, but time and again, they would deliver. Isaacson cites the arresting phrase from Bud Tribble of Apple to describe this ability: "Steve has a reality distortion field," said Apple's Bud Tribble in 1981. "In his presence, reality is malleable. He can convince anyone of practically anything. It wears off when he's not around, but it makes it hard to have realistic schedules."[4] Jobs, in other words, seemed able to distort reality itself, to alter expectations in order to accomplish the company's goals.

We admire figures like Jobs for his drive and discipline. (Actually, I'm not sure I would want to work for him—I like reality just fine the way it is.) For some strange reason, though, when it comes to our faith—the most important thing in this world—we get freaked out if someone talks about discipline. We catch ourselves thinking, *Oh, she just loves rules.* Or *He's a legalist. You can tell.*

As mentioned earlier, it's certainly possible and harmful to think that God accepts us because of our obedience. Legalism is a heresy, and a seductive one at that. Here's the difference between soul-crushing legalism and gospel-driven discipline: legalism tricks you into thinking that certain actions will justify you, or give you righteous standing with God, while gospel-driven discipline makes no such error. It's grounded in the gospel, in the power of Christ's cross and resurrection. It's motivated not by fear or pride, but by the joy set before us that comes from honoring the Lord and doing his will.

So it takes action, but only through and because of Jesus Christ.

I have personally operated by both mind-sets in my spiritual life. I still can! I've read my Bible and prayed in order to accrue some kind of spiritual capital with God, some pious cash in my heavenly bank account. That was wrong, and ultimately neither glorifying to the Lord nor healthy for my soul. I still slip into my old habits, in fact, and I find that when I tend to think according to this pattern, I slip into sin in other areas of life. I justify it— *Sure, this may not be a selfless action, but hey, I had a great quiet time this morning.* I would go so far as to say that I have to regularly remind myself that I don't strive for holiness because I'm checking a box, but because I'm responding to the lavish mercy shown me in Christ.

That's what gospel-driven discipline is: a response. It's hearing from your heavenly Father how incredibly much you're loved, and then plunging into everyday life from that joyful perspective.

That can't be formless or shapeless, though. Godliness is not an invisible, unseen gas. It is a way of life, and it surely includes patterns, standards, habits, and practices that incline you and me to holiness. Your actual decisions will vary on this point, but don't miss the message: if you are going to grow in Christ, you will be forced to act. Sometimes you have to pause your pep talk, roll up your sleeves, and either kill sin or take direct action to grow in godliness.

End of story. No further nuances or qualifications needed.

By the way, all of these actions are valuable *in themselves*, not because others see them. The Lord sees those who "secretly," or privately, obey him, and he is their rewarder (see Matt. 6:4, for example). Don't think an action of the kind I've just suggested is meaningful only if it's public. The Lord sees all your life and all your efforts to grow in holiness. He is pleased by them, and you should seek such growth whether anyone sees or not.

I could sum all of the preceding up by saying this: become

a glutton for maturity. We are encouraged today to think of ourselves as designed for gratification of whatever desire pops up within us. We frequently hear twenty-five-year-olds refer to themselves as "kids"; we hear songs on the radio in which people a decade out of college talk about "staying forever young" and "just having fun." It's easy to think of yourself as a kid today, and to excuse yourself from adulthood and responsibility.

I want to encourage you to think of yourself not as a glutton for indulgence, but for maturity. You and I are like kids cooped up in a classroom all day who can't wait to get out and get some exercise. The Spirit gives us an insatiable desire for discipline and maturity and wisdom. These three ideas are intricately connected, and in remembering how important they are to godliness, I think of the New King James translation of Proverbs 4:7: "In all your getting, get understanding." This speaks to the pursuit of wisdom, and it certainly also speaks to our quest for maturity—as much maturity as you can possibly get, get it!

Once in a while you see somebody win one of those "sixty seconds in a grocery store" contests. The winner gets a cart, races around, and a minute later, that lucky shopper has successfully grabbed 30 boxes of Velveeta Shells & Cheese and 125 refried-bean burritos—all that she could. That's how you and I should think about maturity. Let's get all we can. Let's find joy and excitement in killing the sin that hinders us. Let's find fulfillment not in gratifying our wicked desires but in forging godly habits that stay with us for a lifetime.

As we embrace godly maturity, we won't become perfect. We're going to lapse and fail and get frustrated. We will *feel* our fallenness until the day we die. But the key is this: You and I keep coming. We keep fighting. Forgiveness is real, and grace is more powerful than anything in this universe. We have been freed by God's lavish kindness to see that sin is unsatisfying, and holiness—activated through our focused pursuits—is exciting and life-giving.

As we press on toward a mature Christian life, God will keep growing us.

THE GROWTH AND GOODNESS OF
THE ORDINARY CHRISTIAN LIFE

What have we seen thus far? That you and I are equipped to live as God wants us to live.

This kind of life is not boring or dry. Part of what weakens our resolve is thinking that sin is fun, and holiness, though good, is boring. We look out at the world beyond, at celebrity culture, at Hollywood stars and Hall of Fame quarterbacks, at leading politicians and billionaire playboys, and we think, *Wow—they get to have so much fun. Look at little old me. I'm not doing anything fun. But at least I'm hunkered down for Jesus.* This is a lie! These are false gospels we're believing. They promise satisfaction and create longings in us that we think will be satisfied if we sin and obey them.

But they won't. They will lead us, like the younger brother in the prodigal son story, to chase our passions until they leave us facedown in a pigsty.

Or—here's another possibility—we may not chase those passions, but as Tim Keller has noted, we may end up like the older brother in the same parable, watching the sins of others and justifying ourselves as righteous because we're better than them.[5]

Here's the reality when it comes to satisfaction and happiness: as believers, you and I know the purest form of pleasure there is. Think of Psalm 16:11, which confesses just this: "You make known to me the path of life; in your presence there is fullness of joy; at your right hand are pleasures forevermore." Do you see this? The "path of life" means the way of holiness in Christ—there is life, eternal life, in this way.

It is on this path that one finds "fullness of joy." It is in being a Christian, saved from hell and set free to conquer evil by the liberating Messiah, that we find "pleasures forevermore." We will taste these pleasures forever in the new heavens and the new earth. Life itself will be pleasure, joy grounded in the great kindness of God.

So remember this as you seek to apply what we've talked about in this chapter, as you take practical, daily steps to be a conqueror of evil: Sin is disappointment. Holiness is delight. Honoring God is the most satisfying work you can perform. It leads to God's blessing now—primarily in the form of a victorious Christian life—and it leads to eternal rewards.

When you think about it, this isn't a fair fight.

CONCLUSION

Being a believer does not mean becoming a glow-in-the-dark Christian, hovering six inches off the ground, unaware that a world filled with good food and cool technology and great music and friends exists. It means we exchange small pleasures for big ones, that we embrace the glory of God—and nothing on this earth—as our consuming passion.

So let's not lead our lives as "goofs," whether on the roof, in the library, at the club, or elsewhere. Let's not be mastered by unserious things. Let's not be disciplined in silliness and undisciplined in godliness.

We're not going to be perfect. We're going to fail. All of us. Me. You. Everyone. But let's remember God's power, "which is Christ in you, the hope of glory" (Col. 1:27). Let's be committed to repentance. It's not merely the way we enter the kingdom of Christ—it's the way of life in this kingdom.

We've counted the cost and risked it all to follow the Savior. How amazing that all our investment in godliness will be worth it. Now and in coming days, God will empower us as conquerors for Jesus, making us holier, more disciplined, and much, much happier.

5 RISKY FAMILIES: BUILDING A LEGACY

You live a sweet, little, nerfy life. Sitting on your
biscuit, never having to risk it.

—DARRYL TO MICHAEL, *The Office*

ONE OF LIFE'S JOYS IS WALKING THROUGH A PARK.
Just the thought of it slows my breathing down. I'm writing this,
but now that I've mentioned a nice walk, I'm struggling not to
lose concentration.

Ahhhhh, the park.

Parks are a simple pleasure, and they seem simple in the
making, certainly: you cut some paths, move some trees, and
plant some flowers. Then people walk the grounds, play Frisbee,
battle ants during cookouts, and generally have a nice time.

But it's not so simple, turns out.

This is true whether you're dealing with a small town
park or a massive one, like New York City's Central Park in
upper Manhattan. Millions of people stream into the city each
year, going to Times Square, Broadway, and many other fun

destinations. There is magic in New York City. It's a bit ironic, but no place in this teeming city has more drawn me than the massive park.

A few years ago, I had some meetings in the city and managed to find some time to walk in the park. One enters a different world in stepping into Central Park. If Times Square is New York at work, Central Park is New York at rest. It's a marvelous place, filled with discoveries: a little pond here, an ice cream stand there. One minute you're alone in the forest (an odd feeling in NYC); the next you're feet from a heated Little League baseball game. Ducks make their way throughout; runners shoot by; artists paint portraits for five dollars. All this in a setting that rolls effortlessly on and yields a feeling of peace and solitude.

But that's the thing. Central Park wasn't effortless in the making. It took two of America's greatest nineteenth-century landscape architects, Frederick Law Olmsted and Calvert Vaux, no fewer than fifteen years to design the park. They worked tirelessly on their plans for Central Park; each gave a good portion of his life to the city's capstone preserve. Olmsted in particular crafted a fastidious vision for the park. Flowers and trees should be noticeable, but not too noticeable; paths should be winding in places, but not extreme; ponds should be just the right size. Everything, Olmsted dictated, should be done in proper proportion; the park should not simply run on, but should essentially tell a story for the visitor, one peppered with regular surprises and pervaded by a sense of infinitude. Not for the faint of heart, park designing!

To think—as I did—that parks are just planting flowers here and watering some bushes there. Sorry, Mr. Olmsted!

THE GOSPEL GARDEN

There is a reason that biblical texts like the Song of Songs compare marriage, and by extension the family, to a garden. A family is intended by God's wise design to produce life, to be in the strongest sense a living thing. Families are created by God to pulse with life. They are little solar systems, designed by God to give the full range of human emotions and at the same time to allow us to navigate them.

The family is alive. It's a living thing.

A happy family, with a strong relationship between husband and wife at its core, does not happen by accident. You cannot microwave a marriage, ignoring it one minute then reviving it the next. One builds a strong family through the grace of God and hard work. The family is a huge project, the biggest we can naturally attempt in our lives, because it involves not only the physical creation of those who do not exist, but intense emotional and spiritual bonds between those who do.

Like no other institution in our lives, the family calls for strong commitment. It creates loving attachments, yet on the flip side, we feel incredible pain when those bonds are broken. The creation of any family is a daring enterprise requiring everything we have to give.

You have to risk to build a strong family. You have to trade in dreams of self-driven comfort, ease, quiet, mobility, and indulgence for the self-sacrificial but far more enjoyable goal of leading a family to know and worship God and glorify him together through a happy, disciplined, loving home.

The demands of the family are great. But its rewards are greater. Those called to marriage—and this is most, but certainly not all of us—should contemplate the prospects of a happy life. We may be young, but we should let our minds wander to the close of our lives, where, if God blesses in this way, we sit, holding hands with our spouses around tables filled with happy children and grandchildren (and perhaps some great-grandchildren).

I don't know how these words strike you. Perhaps they interest you, but they don't describe your own experience. You may come from a broken home. You may want to start a family but find yourself unable to. Or perhaps you have started a family, but you don't have a lot of direction for it. Maybe you're single, and called to this role for a lifetime.

Whatever your place in life, as a Christian you have a strong stake in the family. This is true whether you are called to build a family or support one. In the following pages, I want to introduce you to the happiest kind of family of all, the clan created through the power of the gospel and devoted to the glory of God.

WHAT IS A FAMILY, ANYWAY?

I would guess that if you asked many folks what the purpose of a family is, they would focus on things like economic stability, getting kids into college, having good experiences, and so on. Many people, I think, view the family—and beyond this, life itself—in economic and achievement-oriented terms.

It's easy in our age to structure the whole rhythm of the family around money and achievement—to be an *achievement-oriented family*. How? If your first priority is saving up for college and retirement—good things to do!—then you'll naturally make decisions that allow you to reach these goals before others. If you want to reach a certain standard of living, perhaps involving the "American dream" of major savings in the bank, regular vacations, a boat in the yard, two or three cars in the garage, and enough money to play around with, you'll naturally create a day-to-day calendar that leads to such things.

The Christian family is not scared of "success," of money and good education and a two-car garage. These can be great blessings. But it is fundamentally oriented around totally different, and far more important, concerns. The Christian family is all about the glory of God and the spiritual health of the family's members. It is about togetherness and joy grounded in the Lord. It is pursuing something far greater than an impressive pedigree, major high school sports accomplishments, or wealth.

Because of the call to build something greater in Christ, to risk the world to gain eternal life and all its treasures, the Christian family is devoted to God. The family is created *by* God, after all; it is also created *for* God. Every family is designed to be a *worship-oriented family*.

Think about this: God's first creation in the social realm was the family. He didn't first make a government, or an organization, or a village. He brought Adam and Eve together, and in so doing made the first family. Adam received Eve, and the creation of a family, as a great gift: "This at last is bone of my bones and flesh of my flesh" (Gen. 2:24). This is a blueprint for many of us, those who are called to marriage. We see that we, too, were made, not to be alone, but to naturally "fill the earth" by having children and raising families (Gen. 1:28).

The family is not disordered, though. We don't make it up as we go. God establishes a rhythm for the family: the man leads it, protects it, and provides for it, while the woman serves her husband and works very closely with him in a hundred areas to ensure that the family flourishes. Marriage is a picture of the gospel: the husband devotes himself to his wife just as Christ gave himself for the church; the wife cherishes her husband, building him up and supporting him.

Children are seen in Scripture not as a burden, a killjoy, or a barrier to true happiness, but as a great blessing from the Lord. Children have an essential duty to their parents; it's actually a part of the Ten Commandments that they obey their father and mother. And parents have duties to their children. Fathers should "not exasperate" their children, but love them by training them to know the Lord (Eph. 6:4 MSG). In all this, the family consciously worships the Lord and praises his good design, even as the basic rhythms of the home honor him.

The members of the Christian family are meant to be a distant image of the Trinity. The Father, Son, and Spirit aren't merely divine persons who each hang out in their own corner of the celestial realm, keeping to their lonesomes; the Trinity is a family, and the members of the Godhead delight in and love one another. In fact, they even serve one another (John 4:34; 15:26), the Father by leading, the Son by doing the Father's will, the Spirit by operating in the world to accomplish divine purposes. It's just like your family—except everyone is perfect and all-powerful.[1]

BUT . . . AREN'T WE ALREADY DOING THAT?

Maybe you've read what I've just written and think, *Okay, sure. I get that. Cool. I'm good to go, because that's basically what we're already doing: loving one another.*

But here's my guess: many of us may conform to the basic structure I've outlined. I think, though, that it's very easy for worldly thinking to creep into our homes without our knowing it. It's easy for a husband to assume he's loving his wife while she doesn't feel treasured. Yes, he provides for financial needs, and that's terrific. But he seems to care more about his work or hobbies—golf, video games, guitar, computer stuff—more than about her. In other words, he does love his wife in theoretical terms, but he's not living out the *substance* of Ephesians 5:25–28 by sacrificially loving and strengthening her.

A wife can fall into a similar trap. She generally supports her husband, but doesn't really give him much encouragement. She points out his weaknesses and nurses perceived slights. Nobody on the outside could really tell this is the case; she knows how to be "church official" and beam on Sunday mornings as if everything's great. But she's not building her husband up, and so she's not living up to the standard of Ephesians 5:22–23 by sacrificially submitting to him and supporting him.

He's technically loving his wife; she's technically submitting to her husband. But the spirit of the marriage falls woefully short of its structure.

It's easy for both the husband and wife to focus on work over investment in their marriage and time with their children. The husband bears the burden of provision, and he should work hard to free his wife up to love and invest in the children (Titus 2:5; 1 Tim. 5:14). It's a tragedy when spouses never see each other. It's rough on children, furthermore, when they never see their parents. God gives us children to raise them, train them, and love them. Kids aren't little files that we manage, clicking them open now and closing them later when we feel like it. They are an incredible investment.

Many of us struggle to see the blessings before us, though. We're busy, overworked, stressed, overcommitted to sports and extracurricular activities, buried in our phones and games when actually in the same room together, and generally missing the goodness of God's plan for the family.

I know this firsthand. It's not easy to build a family. It's all-consuming work, really. Husband and wife have to be all in. As a husband, you can want to coast, to tune out the cares of everyday life. You don't always want to listen to your wife, much as she needs you; she's raising a legitimate concern about the kids, and your mind is straying to ESPN and other escapes from real life. The kids talk a lot and require constant attention; that's hard! As a wife, you're constantly with your children, so you sometimes feel desperate to get away. You can get short with them. Your husband comes home, and through the fog of tiredness it's easy to focus on his shortcomings and to not be thankful for his work.

You're not some super-deficient family member if these realities resonate with you. We're all sinners. I certainly am, and I have sinful tendencies that God is ironing out. Acknowledging this is a great way to start growing. Personally, I've realized by God's grace that I need to approach family life from a realistic perspective, taking the ongoing reality of sin into account, and leaning on God's grace through prayer to choose a better way than my flesh desires.

The family may be a garden, as we said earlier, but we're a garden with weeds.

A HAPPIER VISION OF THE FAMILY

Your family doesn't have to struggle. Your home can flourish. There is real hope for you and me, wherever we've been or are going.

How can we move ahead? Let me suggest four ways that we can build healthy families. I'm going to work chronologically, starting at the beginning; wherever you are in life, single or married, I think seeing all steps of the plan will be helpful to you because they show the thought *behind* a worship-oriented family.

Prepare for a family as a young single person. God wants us to live according to wisdom. This whole book has operated on that principle. I've taken stories and principles and teachings from Scripture and staked out a basic plan for your Christian life. This is what I think God wants for us. We often think that following God's will is something like chasing a squirrel. You have no idea where it's going; it darts here and there, following no perceptible pattern. It's inscrutable. You can't figure it out; you just chase it for all you're worth.

It's true that no one knows where God will have them go in this life. But that doesn't mean we're off the hook for planning and thinking and building. We've got to mine Scripture for wisdom, pray hard, and then act boldly to win glory for God through a sold-out life. "The heart of man plans his way," Proverbs 16:9 reads, "but the LORD establishes his steps."

So: plan your way. Go with gusto. Trust a great God to establish your steps, to lead you in good paths.

Few areas of your life call more for gospel risk than this one.

You've got to leave behind small, worldly plans, and invest your all in becoming a mature person ready for marriage (not a perfect one, but a mature one). Your parents, really, should be training you for marriage. They should be setting it up as a major mark of maturity. For those called to it, marriage is and should be a goal; it's a project; it's an awesome thing to undertake. It's hard work, and it will challenge you in ways you can't know until you enter into it, but it is a work that takes a lifetime and rewards you in full for that effort.

So set your sights high. Have the goal of building a six-decade marriage. Pray for a spouse, and ask God to give you a union that puts the gospel on display in the midst of a fallen world. You don't merely want to find someone to pass the time with. You want a fellow traveler to love and to go on a great quest with, one that will require the two of you to give every ounce of energy and passion you have to one another.

Seek marriage as a young single person. As a man, you're ready to be married when you can take care of yourself, you can provide for a family, and you're spiritually mature enough to lead your wife to know the Lord better. There's no magic age at which this happens; depending on your background, you may well be ready by your junior or senior year of college, or perhaps soon after you graduate. I know this flies in the face of cultural wisdom today. The average age for a man to be married is about thirty, and for a woman it's around twenty-eight.

Let me get real with you: that's way too old for most of us.

Sexual desire kicks in during the teenage years. There's a lot happening for many of us during the collegiate period, so if we're living responsibly, we're generally able to walk the straight and narrow. But we're kidding ourselves if we think we're going to thrive in terms of holiness if we delay marriage for, say, eight to ten years. This is a recipe for spiritual struggle. And many Christians are using this recipe, sadly.

Time for a narrative change, my friends.

As a woman, it's biblical for a man to pursue you. But that doesn't mean you can't prepare yourself for marriage in all the ways we just covered. You can. You should. It's not realistic to expect that marriage will suddenly appear at your doorstep and all will work perfectly. Hollywood tempts you, especially as a young woman, to think that marriage is all billowing curtains and unexpected romance. With apologies to *The Notebook*, that morally compromised creator of a million breathless hopes, and many a fairy tale, there's some of that, but there's also a lot of hard work and faithful commitment involved in a godly union.

My encouragement: get ready now.

It can be very difficult to be on the side of things that doesn't initiate. But this is a crucial part of biblical womanhood (all biblical Christianity, actually): submission to God's will, waiting on God, trusting a godly man to act, and nurturing him as he does so. Rest assured, though, that the Lord is glorified by expectant trust and much prayer. Of course, it can be hard on the other side too! Guys have to "man up" and approach the girl, after all.

So what needs to happen? A guy gets to know a girl in God-honoring settings; he involves her father or a trusted Christian man (Joshua Harris has written helpfully on how to involve church leaders, if needed, in *Boy Meets Girl*[2]) in seeking permission to intentionally pursue her in a relationship; if she's for it, and things go well, he seeks her hand in marriage, proposing engagement.

Let me give you a little taste for what this can look like. It's my own experience, which isn't normative but may be helpful (and possibly amusing).

In 2005, I met my wife, Bethany, through my seminary professor, evangelical theologian Dr. Bruce Ware. Dr. Ware is a strong leader and brilliant thinker, the past president of the Evangelical Theological Society and the Council on Biblical Manhood and Womanhood. Even more than his pedigree, though, Dr. Ware was a godly man from whom I was learning a great deal.

After Dr. Ware and I talked further about his daughter, I prayed hard and decided to contact her.

It was a good time for all this to happen. In this season of life, it was obvious to me for a variety of reasons that marriage was a good goal. Let's make this brutally clear: I lived in an apartment and used an ironing board for a desk. The nicest meal I could make for myself was mac and cheese with canned green beans and biscuits. I made it all at once and then would have it for three separate meals.

Wife: needed.

We ended up dating/courting (I call it "dateship"—dating for a little while, then seriously entering into what you could call "courtship"); then we got serious. I received permission from her father to marry her. I asked her to marry me, and she said yes. In the summer of 2006, we were married.

God was incredibly kind to me then, as he so clearly is now, and we're in our seventh year of marriage. I don't deserve such a kind, godly, and sacrificial wife.

Our narrative had its own shape, but I want to point out a few things: in an individualistic, hedonistic culture, it is possible to (a) involve the girl's family, (b) be a man in a biblical and traditional sense, (c) care for the woman's heart, and (d) conduct yourself chastely for God's glory. We weren't and aren't perfect people, of course. But God blessed our humble attempts to follow him.

When redeemed sinners take on a great task that glorifies him—like entering into marriage and the formation of a life together—God is kind to lead.

Embrace the blessing of children. Okay. So you're married. What now?

Well, it's no bad thing to have some time together as a married couple to get to know one another and to just plain enjoy wedded love. Marriage is a great gift.

In time, you'll start thinking about children. That's good and right. Some people today don't want kids. They see them as an impediment to happiness. The common mentality among many younger people is basically this:

1. Have fun now (twenties and thirties).
2. Have as many relationships as you want; keep them as minimally defined as possible (if you're a guy, sneeze whenever the topic of serious commitment is raised).
3. Make lots of money and pursue your career with superintensity; alternately, goof off and avoid pursuing anything hard.
4. Eventually, in your late thirties and forties, think about settling down.

Life experiences vary, but there are some weaknesses in this plan. It's tricky for holiness, finding direction in life, and companionship. Plus, it's hard to have tiny kids when you're in your forties (it's hard enough in your twenties!). A common cog in all this thinking, by the way, is the idea that kids are a drag. They aren't.

Yes, parenting is hard work. I'm not going to lie; sometimes you are simply desperate for a night to yourself. Occasionally you're short-tempered. Every now and then you don't want to change a diaper. But here's the thing: being a father or mother is unbelievably rewarding. Dare I say that it's even fun? It's very fun. You and your spouse actually create children together. Or, you adopt children and become their entire world. What is more meaningful than that?

It sounds stereotypical, but you have all kinds of moments as a parent that just slay you in their sweetness. My son randomly comes up and gives me intense hugs that last five seconds. My little girl, as sweet as nectar, recently called the place where you get apples "the apple Richard." Sometimes I look back when I'm driving, and the kids, silently, are holding hands, totally on their own initiative.

I am not kidding when I say that nothing beats such moments. You can have your cocktails and club-hopping. I will take two tiny human beings that are my own, holding hands in the car.

So forget what the culture tells you—you know: that you'll have kids, and that's the end of your life. Besides the gift of a husband or wife, children are God's greatest natural gift to humanity. This is what the Bible tells us. Like Adam shouting for joy over the discovery of Eve, the Psalmist praised the Lord for the blessing of little ones: "Behold, children are a heritage from the Lord, the fruit of the womb a reward. Like arrows in the hand of a warrior are the children of one's youth. Blessed is the man who fills his quiver with them! He shall not be put to shame when he speaks with his enemies in the gate" (Ps. 127:3–5).

When you're ready, build a family as God allows. However you handle timing and planning, let the Word of God, not the culture, shape your mind and thoughts.

Build a loving home devoted to God. When kids do come, they need investment. It will help greatly if you have already invested in your spiritual life. Studying the Bible together, praying together, talking about the sermon together, going to marriage seminars together, going on fun dates a few times a month, and having weekly conversations about how you can encourage one another and kill sin individually will all help you do this.

Some things you can focus on as a young married couple include:

1. Being a good and clear communicator.
2. Creating a spiritually strong environment such that you are consciously devoted to the Lord.
3. Working through conflict in a productive way.
4. Learning how you can love your spouse in ways he or she enjoys.
5. Getting a lot of time together to simply enjoy marriage.
6. Enjoying the gift of sex, which is different from Hollywood's version.
7. Serving your local church and getting to know godly couples in it so you can learn from them.

Building these and other skills will bless you as a husband and wife and prepare you in many ways to be a strong parent.

It's not always easy, as I've said, to figure out how to invest in your children once they come. Modern culture has taught us to prize "quality" over "quantity" when it comes to raising little ones, but this is an unhelpful division. The strongest quality of godly parenting comes when fathers and mothers put in time and effort, and make sacrifices—sometimes big ones—to make that happen. The more quantity of time there can be with one's kids, the greater the chance they will feel loved. With this in mind, read Deuteronomy 6:6–9: "And these words that I command you today shall be on your heart. You shall teach them diligently to your children, and shall talk of them when you sit in your house, and when you walk by the way, and when you lie down, and when you rise. You shall bind them as a sign on your hand, and they shall be as frontlets between your eyes. You shall write them on the doorposts of your house and on your gates."

What does this mean for us? Are we supposed to nail stuff on doorposts? You can if you want. But the point we take away from this foundational text is that we need to constantly train our children to know the Lord, just as the Israelites did. We're called by the Lord to take constant responsibility for our kids, and to teach them by word and deed at mealtimes, at bedtimes, at the park, while driving to the grocery store.

This will naturally mean grabbing time during the day for teaching and investment. Instead of flicking on a DVD in the car, talk to your kids. Memorize a Bible verse with them. Instead of everyone watching TV or playing on their smartphones, gather together at night to read the Bible, talk about it, and pray together. You don't have to be somber about it; there shouldn't be a rule against laughter or fun. Instead of getting too busy and having your kids in one sports league or violin recital after another, cut their activities to a reasonable minimum. Get Saturday back, and go on walks together as a family. Talk about the glories of God's creation.

Godly parenting is not a work you can compartmentalize; it's a calling, a continual calling, and especially so for women, made by God to nurture children (think of Eve being called "the mother of all living" in Genesis 3:20). You have to constantly trade in self-interest for sacrificial love. It's going to be challenging; it's *supposed* to be challenging. It's gospel risk in action, because it means dying to yourself and loving those God has given you. It will take years of commitment and repentance and discipline to do this well, and we'll always see areas of improvement.

But we'll keep going, and keep praying, and keep investing.

This is especially important for fathers. We've got to take our role as spiritual head seriously (see Eph. 5:22–33). Both husband and wife have all kinds of work to do in training their children. The father, however, is the head of his home, the provider, protector, and leader. This means exercising spiritual leadership and helping your whole family know and obey the Lord. That may sound like a huge task. In reality, we can all work our way into it. If you haven't taught anyone theology, and struggle to know where to begin, get a book like *Big Truths for Young Hearts* or *Knowing God*.[3] Read the book with your family for ten minutes at night, discuss it for a bit, and then pray.

These small steps will go a long way toward creating a spiritually oriented home.

BUT WHAT ABOUT SINGLES?

Maybe you've read all this and thought, *That's terrific. But I can't get there. I'm single, and I don't want to be.* How do you build a family in this case?

First, if this wasn't what you thought should happen in your life, you don't have to pretend it isn't challenging. Sometimes you want to get married, but you can't. God does not lead you in this way. If this is so, leave your concerns with the Lord. Pour out your heart to him. Above all else, remember that your sufficiency, your identity, your hope is not a spouse. It is Jesus Christ. All that you need, you have. These are not trite words, but essential ones.

Second, you actually can build a family: a spiritual one. This is the great privilege of all Christians. Through the gospel, and in service to the Great Commission of Matthew 28:19–20, we can "make disciples" of Jesus Christ, bringing people into the family of God. All who confess Christ are "one body" in him (Rom. 12:4–5). The natural family, as we have seen, is given us by God. It is good. But the natural family will give way to the ultimate family, the spiritual one, in the life to come. This is exactly what Jesus said: "For in the resurrection they neither marry nor are given in marriage, but are like angels in heaven" (Matt. 22:30). In the meantime, though, you have the awesome duty of seeing people spiritually adopted into God's family (Rom. 8:1–16). You can find amazing fuel for spiritual work by realizing that you are not in a place of relational suffering—you're freed to serve the resurrected Christ as your married friends are not (see 1 Cor. 7). Like Jesus and Paul, and so many others in church history, you can devote yourself to the Lord in a very practical way.

Third, you can serve the families from your church. They need help. You can play a truly important role by watching the kids and other such tasks that take pressure off of busy husbands and wives. You have a crucial role in being a part of a family-strengthening culture.

Fourth, enjoy the life God has given you. There are tons of things to do. Don't retreat from a full and happy life. Be active; be free; be joyful. Pursue your work and ministry with vigor. Pray for grace when discouragement and regret hit, and know that this is Satan digging at you. God doesn't want you to be sad; he has directed you in the way that most glorifies him, and he wants you to be joyful in him as you travel it.

In these and many other ways you can see your singleness as a gift, not a burden, even as you pray for God's blessing in your life. Some days, it will be easier than others to see this. It may take time for you to own this calling, but God's grace is more than sufficient for our every need. Remember the apostle Paul's words in 2 Corinthians 12:9–10 as he wrestled with his own trials: "But [the Lord] said to me, 'My grace is sufficient for you, for my power is made perfect in weakness.' Therefore I will boast all the more gladly of my weaknesses, so that the power of Christ may rest upon me. For the sake of Christ, then, I am content with weaknesses, insults, hardships, persecutions, and calamities. For when I am weak, then I am strong."

CONCLUSION

We began by comparing the family to a garden. Central Park, I noted, took more than a decade to create. It was not built overnight, contrary to its pleasing natural aura. It took intensive work on a day-by-day basis for weeks, months, and years. Yet almost 150 years later, we're still reaping the fruits of this project.

Similarly, our families are built one day at a time. They require our investment and commitment. We must prioritize them and boldly seize opportunities to grow them. We're going to have to work *against* the culture and our own sin to do so. But the work is all worth it. After all, as believers we're looking toward longer-term blessings.

We're trained in our society to think old people are silly, but when we see a godly couple who has raised a healthy family, it's hard not to marvel at their work. Over decades, through many challenges, they have built something. And all their investment—including the many trials they weathered—was worth it.

The same will be true for us.

6 RISKY WORK: BUILDING A VOCATION

Dear friends, the kingdom of God—and we are that
kingdom—does not consist in talk or words, but in
activity, in deeds, in works and exercises.

—MARTIN LUTHER, 1522 SERMON

MY LIFE CHANGED IN 2005. WHY? WAS IT A MAJOR epiphany? Did someone give me a massive sum of money? Did I go on an overseas trip?

No. It was a then-unknown show called *The Office*, and its razor-sharp, low-key-but-hilarious writing, that changed my life.

The show had so many strengths. It was, in my limited experience, the first comedy that portrayed real people since *The Cosby Show*. It wasn't based on zany events (at least in its first three seasons, which I prefer), but on the ordinary stuff of real life. Everyday existence has plenty of drama, plenty of quiet turbulence, and *The Office* got that. It had a great love story, with Jim and Pam, but instead of some steamy sexual romp, the show (building off of the British version) allowed the halting relationship between noble Jim and double-minded Pam to pick up momentum over time.

In fact, when the two finally married, it was a momentous event. I felt as if good friends of mine had tied the knot. My wife does me one better: she cries whenever she sees it. (Do I get a little salty around the edges of *my* eyes? No comment.)

One thing I do think *The Office*, a show about work, got largely wrong was this though: work. As the show portrayed it, work is something to endure. Get through. Pass. Not really enjoy. Those devoted to their jobs, like Dwight, are weird. The rest of the cast punches the clock, chips away at their duties, cuts some corners, and generally mopes through the day.

Of course, let's be perfectly honest: from a Christian perspective, work can be tough, long, and even dreary. Sin affects work, both in our hearts and as a result of unfairness. We all taste the curse of daily labor due to Adam's sin (Gen. 3:17–19).

But while work is subject to the curse, it's also given to us by God. Adam did work *before* he disobeyed God and brought death to us all (see Gen. 2). It certainly looks as though we will be active in the new heaven and the new earth *after* this world passes away. The apostle Paul urged the Roman Christians to "not be slothful in zeal" but "fervent in spirit" in order to "serve the Lord" (Rom. 12:11). All of life should be marked by fervent hearts, eager to please the Lord in whatever we do (see 1 Cor. 10:31).

That must include work.

SURE, I'LL WORK, BUT . . .

Many Christians, seeing these familiar texts, would agree with me so far. "Yes," you might say, "I'm going to work. I'll make money because I need it for other stuff, including my church." This is a commendable start to understanding and practicing the Bible's bold approach to our daily labor.

But I think there's a great deal more in Scripture to transform our understanding of work.

Many of us, I think, view our faith and our work as largely separate. We go to church and participate in the spiritual work of God; we go to work to make money and do what we do best. The two might overlap—such as when we share the gospel—but are fairly separate.

My generation—twentysomethings and thirtysomethings—has been seriously affected by this mind-set. The problem is not necessarily that we don't want to work. It's that we don't want to really invest in a vocation. We're tempted to be lazy about building a career and finding a calling. Many of us are drawn to less serious things: video games and hangout sessions and shopping and sports and goofing off and social drama. What does this end up doing to us? It makes us approach work lackadaisically. If we're not careful, we can end up trapped in a permanent winter break, with little to do, slightly annoyed parents, and a feeling of aimlessness.

Or, alternately, some of us are tempted to make our jobs an idol, which is an equally harmful pitfall. We were made *to* work, but we were not made only *for* work.

Work does not need to be a bore or an obsession. In the pages to come, I want to give you a healthier perspective on our individual vocation. I think this will have special relevance to believers facing one of three circumstances, which many of us are in:

1. You're in college or just out of it, and you don't know what to do with your life.
2. You've been working for a while but don't know what your career strategy should be.
3. You are struggling to find work in a time that still features a relatively weak economy.

These are different situations that call for unique individual responses, to be sure. But I want to help you see that there is a principle that can help in these instances and many others: God wants you to build a career. He wants you to risk your comfort and ease and boredom and low vocational expectations. He offers you a better, bigger life in his gospel, one that will put every particle of your being to use for his kingdom. The Lord wants you to work for his glory because he's saved you for just that purpose.

Let's talk about how to do that now.

Advance the gospel at work and through work. It is very good to work in full consciousness of the way you bear the image of God. You're not a brute; you're not an automaton; you're not a clump of cells. You have the privilege of knowing that God made you intelligent. God, we see, is the ultimate thinker. He is the Creator, a term we're quite familiar with but which we often think about only when debating evolution. That's a shame.

Christians are sometimes seen as being anti-creativity. We're all about execution and undisturbed order, not the imagination. We like rules, not creativity. But if we're following the example of our Lord, nothing could be less true! We have the *most* foundation for entrepreneurship, art, ingenuity, innovation, and the imagination. We know we didn't come from nothing. We're not cosmic accidents who happen to have ended up as thinking beings.

We are the choicest creation of divine intelligence.

We believe in a triune God who decided to make something from nothing, something so complex we can't ever fully figure it out, something so vast we'll never find its end (see Gen. 1–2). This applies to countless subjects. Think about rain. In detailing God's control of all things, John Piper wrote a fun essay that laid out the intricate process involved in rain falling to the earth from the sky:

> So the sky picks up a billion pounds of water from the sea and takes out the salt and then carries it for three hundred miles and then dumps it on the farm?
>
> Well it doesn't dump it. If it dumped a billion pounds of water on the farm, the wheat would be crushed. So the sky dribbles the billion pounds water down in little drops. . . . How do all these microscopic specks of water that weigh a billion pounds get heavy enough to fall (if that's the way to ask the question)? Well, it's called coalescence. What's that? It means the specks of water start bumping into each other and join up and get bigger. And when they are big enough, they fall. Just like that? Well, not exactly, because they would just bounce off each other instead of joining up, if there were no electric field present. What? Never mind. Take my word for it.

This is too cool for school. To get one tiny drop of rain, a thousand things have to happen in the most intricate ways. God created rain, and with similar ingenuity he created all things. Psalm 104:24–25 hums with praise to the Creator for the beauty, the sheer aesthetic grandeur, of this world: "O Lord, how manifold are your works! In wisdom have you made them all; the earth is full of your creatures. Here is the sea, great and wide, which teems with creatures innumerable, living things both small and great." This psalm isn't just stating the *fact* of creation. It's celebrating the spine-tingling, hair-singeing, mind-exploding intelligence of the Lord.

This should unleash wave after wave of inspiration, creativity, and delight in thinking, planning, strategizing, planning, implementing, and *working*.

This identity, after all, flows from the very first words the Lord says about humanity in the Bible: "Let us make man in our image, after our likeness. And let them have dominion over the fish of the sea and over the birds of the heavens and over the livestock and over all the earth and over every creeping thing that creeps on the earth" (Gen. 1:26). Humans alone bear the image of God. We alone, therefore, can "have dominion" over all the earth, working it, using it for good purposes, building a life from it, honoring God through our earthly labors.

God has commissioned us, in other words, to build and create. We are, if you will, gospel entrepreneurs. Instead of operating in a beaten-down, scared-to-risk, sitting-on-our-hands mentality in which we passively wait for the world to act upon us, we can, like the faithful servants from the parable of the talents, build godly vocations and careers for God's glory. This kind of existence is driven by and dedicated to the gospel. Everything we undertake and create is from the outflow of God's mercy delivered to us by the body and blood of Jesus.

God is pleased, then, by your actual work—by figuring stuff out, troubleshooting, analyzing, planning, ordering, structuring, thinking, and making stuff. He is delighted when you work unto him and find pleasure in your vocation. You are merely doing what he does, after all—working and laboring and creating. This does not apply only to entrepreneurs or artists though; it applies to anyone solving assembly-line problems, fixing plumbing issues, untangling math calculations, teaching children new words, cutting hair a new style, figuring out a better base-stealing method, and too many other work responsibilities to count.

As you think and analyze and make things better, you're showing who you are: a being made in the very image of almighty God.

The Lord is pleased when we work in this way and when we do so as a gospel witness. As we'll talk about in chapter 9, we should see our work environments as opportunities to build meaningful friendships that can introduce those around us to the gospel that has saved us and made us productive and delighted workers. It is good and right to pursue evangelistic friendships in the workplace. Start a lunchtime Bible study with coworkers. Bring a good book to work, and invite discussion of it with fellow employees. Invest in the lives of the people you labor alongside; care about them out of genuine compassion for them, and build toward a full-fledged gospel witness as you are able.

Sometimes Christians in secular workplaces feel bad about not being in "full-time" ministry—but these are the people who by and large have the most opportunities to share the gospel and demonstrate its power by a transformed life. Your work may well be the front-line mission field of the gospel.

If you own a business, furthermore, you can use it to advance justice and goodness in the world. You can make products that help people, or you can set aside time and money from earnings to use for human flourishing and gospel promotion. The founder of Hobby Lobby, David Green, is one example of this. He's bold and on record about using the company for these purposes. He's doing the Lord's work.[2] Sometimes younger Christians might sniff at this mind-set; maybe it sounds pietistic. In my opinion, though, it's honoring to the Lord, and a model for you and me.

Get the relationship between wisdom and God's will straight. Here's the very first thing you need to see as you get cracking on building a vocation: the Lord of heaven and earth is eager for you to boldly work for his glory.

But with that said, we should never think that an active, dominion-taking life is opposed to prayer and trust in God. Wise planning does not cancel out prayer. Instead, prayer drives planning. We pray, seeking God's will for our daily lives, and then we act. Remember Proverbs 16:9? I think it's one of the most important verses in the whole Bible for faithful Christian living: "The heart of man plans his way, but the LORD establishes his steps." This means that we ask God in prayer to establish our steps. And then, being open to his leading, soliciting advice from others, and studying his Word so we'll think in transformed ways, we act. We plan.

We build.

In all of this, God will surely lead us. He is free to correct our paths a little or overhaul them to the max. We hold our fragile lives with open hands. Nothing is promised or owed to us—not wealth, fame, stable families, freedom from suffering, or endless promotions. Everything we have is a gift. To draw breath is a gift. The Lord will do what is best for our good and his glory, whether that means keeping us going in the path we travel or diverting us to some new one. In all this, God's promise to us is that nothing can or will separate us from his love (Rom. 8:31–39).

For a good number of us, life will not be inscrutable, topsy-turvy, and incomprehensible. Many of us will experience God working out his will as meaning a quiet and "normal" life. This will involve building a career. I want to say, very clearly, that such an existence is not sub-Christian or bad.

It is good.

Paul's admonition to the Thessalonians is remarkably helpful on this point: "Aspire to live quietly, and to mind your own affairs, and to work with your hands, as we instructed you, so that you may walk properly before outsiders and be dependent on no one" (1 Thess. 4:11–12).

Here we have Paul praising in strong terms two things: (1) a quiet, ordinary life and (2) daily work. Don't miss the significance of this. All our lives are invested in the most exciting cause there is: the promotion of the gospel of Christ's righteous kingdom. The way we invest in this cause, though, will for many of us mean faithful living in the rhythms of family, home, and work that God establishes in our lives.

What's the point here? Don't see an "ordinary" life as outside the will of God. It actually seems to be the case that God's will works hand in hand with wisdom and even what we could call "common sense" to direct us on the paths He has for us. Even simpler: wisdom and God's will are friends, not enemies.

This is true for your life and mine.

Wisely choose a career that honors God and fits you. Let's take a stroll down memory lane. Sometimes it's tempting to think that the past was perfect and now everything's shot to pieces. Well, that's obviously not the case; the twentieth century saw more people killed by dictators than any other previous century. If life seemed innocent and peachy keen in the nineteenth century, remember that slavery was also legal in many places. We've got to be careful about thinking that the past was less sin-contaminated than the present.

But if you think about how, say, previous generations of Americans thought about their careers, I think you see something healthy. Those setting out to build a career for themselves picked a field that either interested or was open to them. It wasn't super complicated, really. You picked a job and tried to do it well. If it wasn't your cup of tea, you still worked hard—often for years—until you could afford to either switch jobs or start something on the side.

We're in an interesting period today. On the one hand, we're much freer to move to new places and try new things. On the other, we're living in strange economic times, leaving many of us needing more work and without a clear vision for how to move ahead. In such a setting, how do we figure out a plan for our work?

There's no silver bullet, and I'm not an economist. I have great sympathy for those in this spot, and I think many of us will find ourselves in a similar predicament at some point in our lives. There are some questions we can ask, though, in seeking to chart a course for ourselves:

1. What do I like doing?
2. What am I good at, work-wise?
3. Where can I start working at present?
4. Is the work honorable to God? (If no, start over at 1!)

This is rather obvious, I think, but many of us find over time that God has given us our talents and abilities because he wants us, not someone else who doesn't have them, to use them. Put plainly, it's good to use our natural gifts, not bad.

So if you like marketing, get training (and whatever degrees you want) and seek out a job in that field. If you're good at making chairs, be a chair maker. If you like making food, go to cooking school and then become a cook wherever you can. If you're good at starting businesses, or being a personal assistant, or working in the legal field, or investing money, or making flower bouquets, or farming, do that. Without hesitancy. Pursue work that you, to the best of your ability, will enjoy.

Feel complete freedom, as you're praying regularly about this matter, to get counsel from wise Christians who know you. Remember Proverbs 11:14, which reassuringly tells us that "where there is no guidance, a people falls, but in an abundance of counselors there is safety." Talk through with church leaders and friends what you can reasonably hope to do and accomplish. Run everything through the reality test.

The Lord, in my personal example, did not provide for a career for me as a rocket scientist, illustrator, carpenter, or mathematician. In reality, I've always loved writing, thinking, preaching, and teaching, and in his grace, that's what he's opened the door for me to do. It's not that I've arrived vocationally; I haven't. I'm young. I'm still building a career, as you may be. And we all have our days when the universe's alignment feels off. We wonder, *Why are these elements of the job so difficult? What's wrong with me?* That's natural. The curse applies to our work (Gen. 3:17–19).

When we can, though, it's a pleasure to work in a field suited to our gifting and ability. For example, when you see a mother raising her children with skill and grace, it's beautiful. There's such intuition and wisdom involved in mothering and homemaking, as books like Edith Schaeffer's classic *Hidden Art of Homemaking*[3] show. Women working in the home aren't, in my experience and that of many others, bored or unfulfilled. There are almost countless and constantly multiplying matters to handle and solve. It's funny that our modern culture looks down on mothering and homemaking, because in shaping a life and building a loving home, I think the wisdom and ingenuity and energy given us by almighty God is on full and glorious display. What's a more involved "job," and a more significant one, than that?

When I walk past a construction project, I see similar creativity on display. The basic actions that carpenters and builders do without a moment's thought boggles my mind. I'm not an intuitive craftsman. But friends I know can put together, in an afternoon, beautiful cabinetry or woodwork that will last for decades. It's stunning.

Our work puts God's creativity on display. I always loved walking with my father in the woods. He worked as a forester for many years, and so his job was maximally cool: he literally walked in nature for a living. Dad could help a client draw up a plan for management of his lot, knowing intuitively what trees to plan and where to plant them. He could take a plot of land that was overgrown and unhealthy and steward it to health.

The image of God, our fundamental identity, is a mind-blowing reality. God has made us intelligent and creative. He has given us native gifts to use for him, and that pleases him, whether we're world-famous or totally anonymous.

Knowing that transforms our daily labor.

Work hard wherever you are. My wife and I enjoy watching the HGTV channel, which has lots of shows about homes and renovations and redesign. I say I "enjoy" these shows, but mine is a spectator's enjoyment. I have known some of the purest frustration experienced by any member of the human race while undertaking the seemingly simple task of putting together an IKEA chair. (Actually, a good portion of the human race has tasted this frustration. Is IKEA really a home-improvement store, or is it secretly the world's most sophisticated torture device?)

Anyway, sometimes Bethany and I come across *House Hunters*, and the narrative often follows a common trajectory: the house hunters in question regularly want it all. I can hear the voiceover now: *"Newlyweds Bruce and Becky have a $150,000 budget, but they won't stop their search until they find just the right five-bedroom, four-bathroom urban loft with a Jacuzzi and a fully equipped home studio for Bruce's rock band. Can* [insert name of ultra-stressed Realtor looking as though she is being personally hunted by the FBI] *help them, or will this quest burn out?"*

It's not wrong to want a home that fits us. That's a good thing. But I do think we need to be aware of just how entitled we can feel, especially in a relatively prosperous environment. This mentality can easily reach into our daily labor. We think that we shouldn't really take a job unless (1) it's super fun, (2) it aligns with our creative vision, and (3) we aren't "selling out" our integrity.

In different ways, we've been trained today to think that our work isn't important if it's not the song of our hearts, the soundtrack to our souls. It's great to connect your work to your passions; we're crafting a blueprint to do just that in this chapter. But let's be honest: this is not always possible. Furthermore, it can be pretty tricky to pull this off while young. If you're trying to get a career started, your best bet is to get started and work hard.

It's that simple.

This may mean that you're in a field you do not enjoy, frankly. But just working—especially a full-time salaried position if you can get it—will bring tremendous stability to your life. Find work where you can, and do it to the best of your ability. Don't be like some today who set themselves up for disappointment by not really seeking anything definite, or by only lunging at their dream job. If you're stuck, don't accept stasis. Push through it. Be aggressive. Be ambitious.

And don't look down on core benefits of steady work, things like health insurance, a retirement package, and enough money to actually, you know, buy stuff. These kinds of things don't pop up in the flashy media slide shows on the *Fast Company* website. They're vastly underappreciated by many young folks today. It's true that these trappings of stable work are not everything. But they are helpful, especially when you're putting yourself in a position to build and support a family to the glory of God.

So whether you've reached your vocational dreams or not, be grateful for solid employment. Remember that all conscionable work is honorable to the Lord. This is what Paul said: "Whatever you do, work heartily, as for the Lord and not for men, knowing that from the Lord you will receive the inheritance as your reward. You are serving the Lord Christ" (Col. 3:23–24).

Make money to the glory of God. Two questions:

1. Have you ever heard of Henry Parsons Crowell?
2. Have you ever eaten Quaker Oats cereal?

Let me guess your answers: no to the first, yes to the second. Or at least you've heard of the second. I enjoy Quaker Oats, myself. I feel like a grandfather saying that, but it's true. I can't lie.

Why are we talking about cereal? Because Henry Parsons Crowell founded Quaker Oats. I don't know about you, but I love reading about entrepreneurs' visions, leadership, and creativity. Crowell is an unknown guy today, but he was a dynamo in his day. Born to a Christian family in 1855, he overcame tremendous odds as a young man after falling ill with tuberculosis. He eventually bought the defunct Quaker Mill factory in Ravenna, Ohio, and along with it the trade name "Quaker" (though he was not a Quaker).

Over the next several decades, Crowell applied his business ingenuity to what became the Quaker Oats Company. By 1920, his company had made $120 million in revenue, in part due to its Puffed Rice and Puffed Wheat products (that's well over a billion dollars in today's currency).[4] In taking a once-dead company to global success, Crowell had become fabulously wealthy, but he defied the way of the world. He had committed his earnings to the Lord and tithed around 70 percent of his earnings in adulthood.[5] A huge portion of his giving went to the Moody Bible Institute, but Crowell didn't stop there. He helped the school develop its radio ventures and later its renowned aviation program. These were no small contributions—even a century later, MBI has more than four hundred affiliates, and it has sent many thousands of graduates to the mission field, among other places of ministry.[6]

What's the point here?

The point is that Crowell made a lot of money, but he didn't make it for himself. He genuinely believed he could serve God by using his entrepreneurial gifts to advance the gospel of Christ's kingdom. There was a marvelous synergy in his life, in other words. His brilliant marketing wasn't separate from his simple piety.

I want to be frank: some Christians may have a problem with all this talk about huge amounts of money. It's certainly good to be on the alert about the temptation of riches. The love of money really does stimulate all kinds of evil desires and actions (1 Tim. 6:10). And the Bible commends lusting after neither poverty nor riches (Prov. 30:8). It's notable to us that Judas sold out Jesus not for fame and glory, but for a bag of money. What could be more evocative of the temptation of riches than that?

But let's strive to be careful and nuanced in our thinking. The Bible doesn't enfranchise "prosperity theology," but neither does it support so-called poverty theology as a way of life for the majority of God's people. Some today think it's especially spiritual to opt out of the market, renounce one's possessions, and live hand to mouth. That's what you do if you're really, truly godly. I disagree. Some are no doubt called to undertake some version of this way of life. We support many missionaries, for example, who raise support to take the gospel of Christ to lost souls. Our giving should be generous, sacrificial, and joyful. But that means that many of us actually need to lead money-producing lives. We need to tap our God-given skills to create wealth. We need to labor hard and well at jobs that aren't explicitly spiritual in order to bless our families, our churches, and the global missions effort.

As we work hard and wisely, we do well to remember Paul's words to Timothy in 1 Timothy 6:17–19: "As for the rich in this present age, charge them not to be haughty, nor to set their hopes on the uncertainty of riches, but on God, who richly provides us with everything to enjoy. They are to do good, to be rich in good works, to be generous and ready to share, thus storing up treasure for themselves as a good foundation for the future, so that they may take hold of that which is truly life."

Paul does *not*, in this passage, malign wealth, possessions, or even what you might call a "nice lifestyle." He does not condemn the rich. He does not castigate them for their wealth. Instead, he calls them to do two things: to remember the ultimate end of life, God and his glorification, and to be positively sacrificial in the way they live, to be "rich in good works."

So what does this mean for us when it comes to basic needs and even wants? Can we buy cars or houses or air conditioners or running shoes? In answering this question, perhaps we should consider a few biblical figures made wealthy by God.

- Abraham had tremendous land holdings and possessions, including "gold" (Gen. 13:2).
- Joseph was elevated to power, major influence, and tremendous wealth by God (Gen. 40–41).
- David knew fantastic wealth as the king of Israel, as God hugely blessed his reign (1 Chron. 29:8).
- Solomon's wealth surpassed that of all other earthly kings (2 Chron. 9:22).
- Job was a man of superlative wealth both before *and* after calamities befell his family (Job 1, 41).
- Joanna, wife of Chuza, knew great wealth due to the fact that her husband was the steward of Herod Antipas, king of Galilee; she used the wealth to fund the apostles' gospel work (Luke 8:3).
- The Ethiopian eunuch and the Roman centurion who came to faith were both high-ranking leaders and likely wealthy (Acts 8, 10).

Being godly does not necessarily mean you will be wealthy. God makes no such guarantees in the Bible. But as this brief list shows, God is clearly not opposed to wealth, even tremendous wealth. He is pleased to grant it to some of his followers. This means, I think, that he is not opposed to what you could call a "normal" lifestyle. If we're giving sacrificially out of love for Christ from our earnings, and living wisely, I believe God is pleased with us.

There's no exact biblical figure here for New Testament Christians; scholars such as D. A. Carson suggest a general principle of sacrificial generosity to our churches, global missions, and needed cultural endeavors.[7] Personally, I think devoting 10 percent of our earnings to our church and the global missions cause is a good starting point, and we could increase that by a percentage point each year if possible.

So give richly, and avoid false guilt. It's not wrong to spend money. Cars, coats, paved driveways, dark chocolate raisins, and good books can all be good common-grace gifts of God. Vacations aren't wrong, provided they're not what we live for. Treating one's family well as a provider is a delight. And as a worker, you should feel free to make money aggressively in ethical ways. Be shrewd in your business. Apply all your abilities and talents to work, creativity, and entrepreneurship. Enjoy the life that God has graciously given you.

For many of us, we'll see over time that when God came to us and called us to count the cost and follow him, he did not abandon us. He asked us to give up the world, and by his power, we did. From there, he blessed us in all kinds of ways, none of which we deserved.

In other words, all the risks his gospel asked us to take were worth it. We lost the world, and gained everything in Christ (Rom. 8:32).

CONCLUSION

Let's return to my love for *The Office*. Its early seasons are often rich, funny, and even insightful about life in a fallen world. It is right that work can be long and taxing and even frustrating. You know this; I know this. We all have different duties to perform in our vocations that aren't our personal favorites. I certainly do. Let's not kid ourselves: it will always be that way. Because of the curse, work is hard.

I do have one major bone to pick with the show, though: while we all understand the tough parts of our jobs, *The Office's* approach to work boils down to *get through the day. Slog through life. Do anything to burn the time, including the Office Olympics.*

If we will adopt biblical categories, we can punch the gas, not the clock. We can build something invigorating. We can dream big, make bold plans, and aggressively pursue a vision for our lives that makes maximal use of our God-given gifts and passions. God has given us the opportunity to work not for temporal, fading things, but for the advancement of the gospel of his kingdom. When we use our gifts, and when we speak and act in our vocations as distinctly gospel-captivated people, we do just that: we advance his reign and rule.

7 RISKY CHURCH: BUILDING A GODLY COMMUNITY

We need a generation ready to go. . . . A generation
bold enough to say, we are going to show what
Christianity really looks like.

—ALBERT MOHLER, MESSAGE ON CHURCH PLANTING

EVERY ONCE IN A WHILE, YOU COME ACROSS A PIECE OF
writing that shocks you. I had that experience not long ago when
I was flying around the web and came across an article that
stopped my Internet surfboard in its tracks. It was titled "I Fell
in Love with a Megachurch." But it wasn't posted on the website of *Christianity Today* or something expected like that. It was
on *Salon.com*, one of the most "progressive" sites on the web.
But things only got stranger. The author, a twentysomething
named Alexis Grant, hadn't "fallen in love" with any old megachurch though: she was swept up by Lakewood Church, site of
prosperity-gospel preacher Joel Osteen.

You can't make this stuff up.

Here's what Grant said began to draw her to Lakewood:

At Lakewood, emotion pulsed through the crowd. People sang loudly, with both hands outstretched, palms toward their God as if to receive whatever he offered. I put my hands out too, feeling sheepish, glancing around to see if anyone could tell I was a newbie. Soon the whole place was jumping up and down and belting the lyrics, "I'm Still Standing." (Think worship lyrics, *not* the Elton John song.) As they waved their arms in the air, I hoped their strength would rub off on me.

Grant enjoyed many aspects of the services. But she found more "motivation" than religion at Lakewood:

Lakewood felt more motivational than religious—or maybe that was simply what I wanted it to be. Ironically, the secular spirit that drew me there was exactly why some religious folk criticized Osteen: They complained he wasn't religious *enough*. When Osteen did invoke religious images or drift into Jesus talk, I'd tweak his words so they worked for me. He said things were in God's hands; I heard it as fate's hands. He said God would send luck my way; I told myself to make my own luck. By performing this sort of calculus, I managed to convince myself that I wasn't becoming one of those religious nuts.[1]

This is interesting material on its own terms. A skeptical, highly educated journalist, trained at an elite college (Colby College in Maine) to distrust many of the things Protestantism represents, finds herself . . . *enjoying* a therapeutic megachurch that preaches the prosperity gospel (not the true one)?

It's an odd scene any way you slice it.

WHY THE CHURCH, BRO?

Do you know what this poignant episode shows us? It shows us that we need the church. Sometimes we substitute "community" in that last sentence. We need "community." Well, there's truth there. But you know what you and I really need? We need the church. It's the ultimate community, created by almighty God so that people like you and me can flourish, laugh, learn, grow, weep, and love Christ together.

We're not meant by God to be lone rangers. We're made to plug into the fabric of a living body, one aimed not simply at life change or communal uplift but at the glory of God.

Coming to a church, a group of believers covenanted together in the name of Christ, is like happening across a crowd of people on a sidewalk. They're all staring upward. They see something that is clearly blowing their minds. Maybe their hair is standing on end. You ask them who they are and what they're doing, and they reply, "Seeking God." Okay, so the analogy's mildly weird, but that's the point: this is a group of people who are zeroed in on transcendence. They're not content to talk about it in their dorm rooms or book club. They can't just name-check the Lord or wear a "Jesus piece," as Kanye West does. They are compelled by something in them, something mysterious, to worship God.

But that's the crazy thing: they don't want to do it by themselves. They have an insatiable appetite to get together with other people and worship God. Is that merely a natural instinct? You know: if we're going to be outside burning sticks, trying to heat our dinner over an open flame, we may as well congregate?

We're by nature sociable as humans, but there's something more happening in the church. Our instinct for togetherness comes directly from that same source we were just talking about: God. More specifically, a trinitarian God. The Father, Son, and Spirit are the central reality of Christianity. The three persons of the Godhead are each fully God. There is nothing lacking or incomplete in any of them. Yet in a way that is thoroughly brain-bending, they *want* communion with one another. They don't each rule a separate part of the universe; they live in perfect harmony with one another, loving one another, agreeing with one another, manifesting their glory together.

Maybe you're thinking, *Whoa! We just went from 0 to 60, dude. First we're talking about some church; now we're on the deepest mysteries of the universe?* Yeah. Kind of. But this link makes sense. We want to be together as humans because the persons of the Trinity are together as God. We're the image of God, remember? The society of heaven has created a society on earth. We were made for communion and friendship and happiness and perfect love, because that's what the Trinity experiences.

So that, my friend, is why we want a church. We're social beings, like the Father, Son, and Spirit. We're made for the church. We don't just want togetherness; we want togetherness based on the best thing there is: God. We *want* to worship something. We were made for this purpose. God didn't just want his creatures to scurry all over the place like human ants. He made us to crave, love, desire, yearn, delight in, and enjoy him.

Passion is infused in us. Love is hardwired in us.

We're made to adore, celebrate, and shout as loud as our lungs will allow, "I LOVE YOU!" And we're made to do it together, as a church.

In this chapter, we're going to look at how you can help build a local church, whether an existing one or a new one. You know what this is going to involve, right? It's going to mean that you need to risk. You need to give time, effort, energy, love, and commitment to your church. You're going to have to take the step of trusting people and getting connected to them. You'll have to abandon self-protectedness and self-centeredness, and embrace community life. You'll need to invest your passion in the church, a group of people the world will not encourage you to think of as worthwhile.

Let's now plot a strategy for doing just that.

Love God and the church. Here's an interesting reality: lots of people want to love God today. That's what they say. Check out the polls regularly printed in *USA Today*, for example, and you'll find that most people are not in fact hardened secularists waiting to pounce like a hyena on any Christian they can find. You may pick up that impression from the news media or talking heads on TV, but that's not how many people represent their desires. Many folks want to get in touch with God. Of course, they don't know how, and many don't really follow through. Without God's redeeming grace, our sin gets in the way of our best intentions.

But the point stands: a good number of folks would at least say that they want to love God. I think you would baffle many people, though, if you extended the question to this: "Do you want to love the church—an actual, real, existing local church in your area?"

It's at this point that a lot of people would drop out. They would argue that they're "spiritual," but not really religious. They believe in a living relationship with the Lord, not a ritualistic one. They can worship God anywhere, and they don't need to be confined to a building.

Perhaps, in fact, this voices your perspective. Maybe you've been burned by a church. You *don't* associate the local church with a place of joyful worship where you encounter the transcendent Lord of heaven and earth. In fact, there are so many people who have had negative experiences that I think it's worth saying what the church is not:

1. The local church is not a social club for gossip, albeit with pews and a slightly odd smell.
2. It's not a place where you go to observe a whole bunch of weird rules that have no connection to everyday life.
3. It's not a political organization dedicated to the preservation of "what America used to be" or to a social agenda overturning traditional American ideals.
4. It's not primarily about feeling better, thinking more positively, achieving your best self, spiritually "winning," or getting healthier.
5. It's not a building, a place where some people go during the week to observe some old rituals that nobody really understands but that are considered valuable because they create togetherness and make people feel spiritual.
6. It's not a place where people who look like one another congregate and do all they can to keep others who aren't like them out.
7. It's not a spiritual smoothie bar where you go when you have a sudden and unexplainable rush to get close to God, only never to return.
8. It's not a money-raising organization or a series of weekly seminars on success. The church is not a personal improvement organization such that you can climb the

economic ladder, get better jobs, and become fabulously wealthy just by going there.

These are eight ways of thinking about the church that people adopt today. They all fall short in different ways of what it actually means to love God and his church. You may have experienced some form of these conceptions of the church. You may have gone to a church that was all about rules, for example, or that never really preached about the Bible.

A church may have legitimately angered you, offended you, hurt you, confused you, or bored you. I don't know where you're coming from, but I know that no local church is perfect, and that there are many places that are not true churches that nonetheless call themselves by this weighty name.

But what is the local church, then? Well, first and foremost, it's a group devoted to worshiping the living God according to his inerrant Word, the Bible. It's an outpost for weary people burdened by sin to meet God and be transformed by him. The church building may not look exciting from the outside, or it may be an aesthetic masterpiece. Whatever the building looks like, though, I can assure you that the local church truly is exciting, because when it's devoted to God's Word, it is the body of Christ. It's a tangible, visible sign that God is real and working and moving in our world.

You could say it this way: the church is *created* by the gospel, and the church is *edified* by the gospel.

God loves the local church. He made it, after all. It's his brainstorm. God is super-creative. He's the ultimate aesthete. He loves beauty and full-orbed, surround-sound faith. He wants all our senses and emotions to be engaged in weekly worship. So we pray, sing, hear the Word read and preached, eat the bread and drink the wine, and share fellowship together.

The Lord wants these blessings for us. We experience them when we join local churches (see 1 Cor. 5 and its discussion of those "outside" and "inside" the Corinthian congregation). What's called "church membership" is very important in Scripture. Our redeemer wants every born-again Christian to be in fellowship with others so we can build one another up in the faith. He wants us to be baptized as our public declaration that we've passed through the waters of judgment and have risen from spiritual death through Christ. He wants us to partake of the Lord's Supper to remember Jesus' death on our behalf.

I didn't grow up in a massive congregation. I grew up in a small church on the coast of Maine. There weren't many believers around. But I was trained to see the church as an inherently dignified gathering regardless of how many people attended on Sunday. My father was steadfastly committed to the First Baptist Church of East Machias. He went every week to prayer meeting; he and my mother were faithful to the church even through troubled times. They modeled covenantal commitment to their church. I am grateful they did.

It made a mark on me.

Church was a natural part of my youth; without really knowing it, I was formed in the worldview we're discussing here. I was being trained in the holy rhythms of a Godward life. I heard the preaching; ate the tiny little communion crackers barely visible to the human eye; sang in the Christmas choir. We weren't a large body, but we were devoted to the Lord.

More important, he was devoted to us.

He is devoted to every church, to every local expression of

the global people of Christ, however humble, however popular. So should we be.

Be honest about, and committed to, the church. Let's press pause for a moment; this commercial break is sponsored by Rugged Honesty. Occasionally, if we're being truthful, church can be tough. Our workweeks are long; Sunday comes along, and we don't exactly spring out of bed. It's not that we begrudge the Lord the worship due him. But we're fallen people. We're tired.

This is true of many of us. I have been blessed to be a member at great churches over the years, but there are a few days a year when—even at the richest of congregations—your will has to lead your heart. Admitting that isn't wrong; it's part of acknowledging our frailty, our un-Godness. We're not God. We're not perfect. Life isn't always easy. God can speak, and a universe beams with life and light. You and I, though, are not God. We are not omnipotent. We are not perfectly righteous.

My wife is a very gifted pianist. It's very clear to me, without any hyperbole, that part of God's gift to her is unusually expressive and elegant musical ability. I hear her play, and I feel as though I'm seeing unusual intelligence at work. She and I love that she can serve our vibrant local church by playing in the worship team. So she does. On Sunday mornings when she leaves early, I'm in charge of getting the kids to church on time (and, perhaps more elementally, alive). It calls forth all my energies and so I am reminded because of God's lavish love for me to be thankful.

If we're honest, I think we know that we know that we all need to strive for joy, however fulfilled we may be and however happy our church is.

We're going to face these realities until we are glorified and we lose our frailty, sinfulness, weakness, wandering hearts, restlessness, boredom, and laziness. If we embrace this truth, we free ourselves up to cut through our excuses. We're then able to see how good the gospel is for us. We're prepared to cling to it, to know that God has given us the power through Christ's cross and resurrection to keep persevering, and to love those God has placed by our sides as fellow members. This power to love is stronger than our fallenness and weakness. It has overcome our fragility (see 1 John 3). Jesus, as he did with the sick and blind and dead, has restored us. We may not *feel* that he has; but we can *know* he has.

There's more. We're now empowered to obey God through the Spirit. Contrary to our "spiritual, but not religious" age, we know that love is demonstrated through action. We love God. And so we gather together. We push through our tiredness. We pray for power, and then we let the Spirit speak life into our bones.

You know what we so often find? That God is pleased to renew us, and to give us a fresh sense of the goodness of his church, which is for us and our growth in godliness.

Get the right perspective on serving the church—and then serve it. Let's illustrate this next point with an illustration from the world of . . . skiing! (I love skiing.)

I remember skiing as a child on the pristine slopes of Maine. It was a blast, but it was frightening at times, especially when we got up on a Black Diamond trail (they're very challenging). We would get off the chairlift, and I would go into serious snowplow mode, going as slow as humanly possible. This was especially true when I went over ice. The reality of skiing over ice is this: there is no safe way to navigate it. You just have to speed over it.

I can remember skiing down trails at snail speed, faster skiers whipping past me, my goggles fogging up.

Not for nothing did Jack London set his classic survival tale, *Call of the Wild*, in the world of snow.[2]

But here's the thing: when you do acquire the skill and expertise necessary to stop snowplowing and start skiing parallel (putting your skis together for maximum speed), all of a sudden it's as if you're in a different universe. You've entered *pure speed*, the video game-like skiing experience in which you whip down the trail, feel your stomach drop as you soar off a jump, narrowly avoid overhanging trees, hold your breath as you skate over pure ice you hadn't seen a second earlier, tuck your body as low as it will go, and roar into the chairlift line at the end of the trail, ideally spraying any available family members with as much snow as possible.

When you're skiing in cold places like Maine, you need hand warmers. They are miracles in plastic packages. You put them in your ski gloves, smush them around, and minutes later, your hands are roasting. It lasts for ten to fifteen minutes, maybe; then the heat subsides.

How does skiing intersect with the local church? Well, the local church isn't supposed to be a spiritual hand warmer. You're not supposed to get momentarily warm and fuzzy about the church, only to grow cold. You're supposed to commit to the church. You could even say this: you're called to help build the church.

But what does this look like?

Service in our local churches should proceed from love of God and therefore joy in God. This is a crucial point: if we say we want to serve the Lord, then we shouldn't excuse ourselves from the church. We should see the local church as the *first* place we go when we want to honor him by service. Loving God in spirit and truth means loving flesh and blood.

As you think about service, keep in mind what we said earlier: it's not always easy, or the most natural thing, to want to serve right here and right now *with this congregation*. This mind-set will pop up, I assure you, at some point in your church involvement. Knowing that can ward off a lot of discouragement.

In light of this reality, we need to remember the example of Jesus if we're going to serve God's people. Loving God, for Christ as for us, meant loving sinful people. Jesus had infinite reasons for drawing back from those who followed him. He was God, after all, and he knew what was in the heart of humankind. He knew our selfishness, our greed, our pride, our jealousy, our competitiveness, and our self-absorption. And yet he did not withdraw. He was not diffident. He was not detached from ordinary people. He plunged into the fray, if you will. He humbled himself out of pure love for God and man and did nothing else but serve. He devoted his entire life to it.

But Jesus wasn't merely a man of impressive character. He gave himself up to death in the act of ultimate service (1 John 3:16). His self-sacrifice brought salvation to wicked people like us who can do nothing, absolutely nothing, to save ourselves.

That's the image we need to keep in mind for bold commitment to our churches. Building your local church, strengthening and nurturing it, doesn't proceed out of a pragmatic desire to help. It emerges from a heart full of love for God and a mind ablaze with knowledge of what Jesus did to serve.

With this foundation in place, let me give you some thoughts on how you and I can serve our churches. This is just a start:

1. Be a part of the worship team. Leading people in song is a very meaningful part of the weekly service.
2. Clean the church building. People tend to overlook this kind of service, but who wants to attend a service in a dirty building? This is a huge way to serve.
3. Greet people. It's a blessing to have folks say hello to you. Small forms of human contact matter a great deal.
4. Lead a Sunday school class. Church members and visitors alike can get a ton out of a well-done class. You can learn biblical truth, ask questions, and discuss tough matters.
5. Host a small group. Opening your home to members of your small group and shepherding them through a book or biblical text will help them to learn God's Word and to be loved by God's people.
6. Cook meals for new moms, elderly members, or anyone, another form of service that's overlooked but deeply appreciated.
7. Competently run the sound for the service. If the mic isn't working, nobody's happy. We've all been to events where the sound guy is overmatched. The speaker opens his mouth and—*BOOM!* An explosion to lose your teeth by. Either the Transformers are battling Megatron, or the sound guy's out of his depth.
8. Teach a kid's class or volunteer for the nursery. There are few experiences that are more spiritually refreshing than being able to sit in a church service with one's spouse, without worrying about the baby crying.
9. Visit and write notes to shut-ins. Some of my most indelible ministry memories are in nursing homes,

      witnessing people who are close to the end singing
      praise to Jesus.

10. Mentor and disciple a child. With proper setup that
      legally protects you and the needy child, identify a boy
      or girl who doesn't have a father or mother. Give him or
      her the chance to spend time with your family.

11. Count and help manage the church finances. This
      is easy to overlook, but it's one of those departments
      in church life that threatens disaster if someone's not
      serving.

12. Be part of the evangelism team. The church needs
      people to make contact with unbelievers. This is super-
      important work (we'll talk more about this in chapter 8).

We're just scratching the surface with these ideas. I hope
what you see, though, is that there are countless ways for you,
with your particular interests and abilities, to bless your congregation. Every member is equipped for ministry. The Spirit
dwells in all of us, and Christians are a "kingdom of priests"
(Ex. 19:6; see also 1 Peter 2:9). Every single person, not just a
pastor, serves the Lord and ministers in his name. There may
well be less tangible, less defined ways that you plug into and
love your local church. If so, great! Faithfulness does not equal
program participation. It equals gospel-inspired love for the
church and also, secondarily, those beyond it.

I grew up under a Sunday school teacher named Elsie
Dennison. She was a widow. She was about seventy when I first
met her, and she faithfully taught the children's class. She was a
sweet Christian woman, and I can still remember some of her
teaching. Probably the earliest understanding I received of God's

love for his children from the foundation of time was her giving all of us kids an envelope. In each envelope was a little piece of paper with the kid's name on it. Miss Dennison told us that if we loved Jesus, our names were written in the Lamb's Book of Life by God himself. It was a simple exercise, but it made a mark on me.

Countless Christians like Elsie Dennison serve the church. No one knows their names. But their service is honorable, meaningful, and pleasing to the Lord. It builds and strengthens the congregation, and it glorifies God. This is a life-transforming reality.

All this is true whether you serve an existing church or help "plant" a new one in order to reach lost people in your community. Whether you're in leadership or not, you have a tremendous opportunity as a believer to serve that body in all kinds of ways. Building into an existing congregation is terrific. Perhaps there's a flagging church in your area. It's small and doesn't have a ton of energy. Maybe you can be a part of reviving that assembly. Maybe that's your call—to come alongside those believers, serve with them, encourage them, promote gospel teaching at that place, and work to stir it to life. This is an honorable, meaningful thing to do, whether or not the church sees outward success.

Or perhaps you help in some way to plant a church in a needy area. Whether you're the lead pastor or a contributing member, you have a tremendous chance to "build" a new work of the gospel. The building, dominion-taking mind-set applies to all churches, and those involved in church plants will no doubt feel the contours of this mind-set keenly as they set up chairs, put out the coffee, call guests who filled out visitors cards, and pray together for the Lord to send his Spirit in a given place and draw needy sinners to the church.

There has been a renaissance of church planting in recent years. It is personally exciting to me to hear of churches beginning all over the world where they have not existed. Being a pastor of a plant or a core member will very often mean personal sacrifice. It can look exciting on paper but can be hard in reality. There are few things that a Christian can do that more honor God's biblical call to invest our talents than to start a Bible-preaching congregation in a dark place.

Both church revitalization and planting are good and needed forms of gospel ministry in this country and around the world. Every church, furthermore, needs godly members, or it will suffer; being part of a healthy congregation, and building into it, is a wonderful call. In an age of unchallenging Christianity, when broader vision is sorely lacking, we need Christians who will intentionally set out to either strengthen an existing congregation in order to advance the kingdom, or begin a new church that will reach out to people and bring them into fellowship with the living God.

Whether or not we actually go somewhere to carry out this work, we can all be a part of giving sacrificially to this form of ministry, with an eye for unreached places and people. Doing so follows the example of apostolic ministry (see Paul's words in Philippians 4:16–18, for example).

Support your church's leadership. God loves leadership. He is the ultimate leader, and he has structured his church to be led by godly believers.

The church should be led by elders, men of character and teaching ability (1 Tim. 3:1–7; Titus 1). They provide spiritual oversight, leadership, and teaching. Their ministry is supported by deacons, who ensure that the practical needs of the congregation are met. (See 1 Tim. 3:8–13 for the qualifications of deacons.) God has given these offices to the church so it can be ordered, healthy, protected, and strengthened. Every church member is called to submit to their church leadership. This doesn't mean mindless emulation; obviously, if an elder or pastor (the terms are synonymous) seeks to lead the church into sin, it must not follow. But this principle does mean that we give thanks to God for our leaders, encourage them in their godly work, and support the ministry they're leading.

We can all think of assemblies of God's people that were torn apart by a lack of love between leaders and people. Satan hates God's church (see 1 Peter 5:8). He wants nothing more than to place sinful dynamite in it by creating tension, spreading gossip and slander to light the fuse, and then blowing the whole place up in spectacular and maximally public fashion. A major way he accomplishes this end is to pit leaders against members. Leaders, of course, must not oppress or mislead the people of God. Members must not despise or be jealous of or slanderous toward leaders.

A huge means, by the way, of encouraging leadership (and fellow members) is simply this: attend your church's services and functions. Be as faithful as you can. Some seasons in life are tougher than others—when you have young kids, for example—but every member can fundamentally bless his or her church by being *at it* and communing *with it*, as Hebrews 10:24–25 encourages us: "And let us consider how to stir up one another to love and good works, not neglecting to meet together, as is the habit of some, but encouraging one another, and all the more as you see the Day drawing near."

Don't underestimate the power of being together, and of acting in commitment to your congregation. It may seem small, but it will be a major blessing to your leadership and your fellow members.

See the church as a place of joy and courage. We covered some stereotypes of the church earlier. It's pretty clear that some people will struggle to see local churches as, well, joyful places. As I pointed out previously, it's understandable that baggage in our past will affect the way we view the church. Of course, even baggage doesn't excuse our own sin; we're not off the hook of God's justice, in other words, if someone has, say, been unkind to us. We're all desperately wicked; we all in different ways suffer the consequences of human depravity, whether our own or that of others.

There's so much we could say about what the church is and should be. Though we have to omit some material, we can't leave out how we should view the church. Gospel-preaching congregations should fundamentally be joyful assemblies. Our primary demeanor should be one of delight. We shouldn't primarily be known for how grim we are, for how little fun we have, for how many rules we follow, for what we teach people they can or can't do. We should be marked as a people of joy. When we say to the supermarket clerk that we're members of an area congregation, he or she should instinctively think of us as people who seem oddly delighted by God.

That's what we want our identity to be.

This kind of culture is created by what we talked about toward the beginning of this chapter: seeing that the church is all about God, and that we are a part of it not primarily out of duty but because of love. When this—and no other competing reason—is our motivation for our weekly involvement, then joy will naturally flow from our time together, and mark our lives.

When we're joyful and satisfied in God, we are freed to build a strong life together. This will necessarily involve killing sin as a community. Killing sin will mean speaking hard truths in gracious words. We need to be courageous in our churches. We can't paste on a big smile when we gather together and act as if everything is fine. Sin is real, and it's going to affect us until we die or Christ returns. We've got to confront it, first in our own spiritual lives (see chapter 4), then in our families, and then in our churches.

This doesn't mean being the holiness police. We've got to carefully consider when to speak up and exhort a brother or sister in the faith (see Gal. 6:1). But it does mean being courageous to oppose Satan and aid one another in the fight for purity. God doesn't make us "conquerors" to stand alone and detached; he brings us to one another's side and makes us a company of victorious warriors against the kingdom of darkness.

And it means evangelizing continually, striving to bring lost souls, just as we once were, into the fellowship of God's people. The church will be joyous, surely, as it honors the Great Commission and shares the gospel with people in the community. Not every church will grow at breathtaking rates; many assemblies experience ups and downs over the years. Endurance and faithfulness are key, though our zeal for evangelism is never driven by "results" or our "success."

We want to build the church, so we cannot help but share the gospel and live it out. This itself is a joy, and it will bring joy.

CONCLUSION

We started this chapter with a gifted woman who ventured into a megachurch. With you, I pray that friends like Alexis Grant, the journalist from *Salon*, finds Jesus.

I recently heard another story of a gifted woman who ventured, against all the odds, into a church. Her name is Rosaria Champagne Butterfield. Her story is extraordinary. Some years ago, Butterfield was a lesbian in a committed relationship. She was a tenured professor of English and women's studies at Syracuse University; in other words, she had advanced to the top of her field. She had a wide platform for her views and was an unabashed activist for the spread of homosexuality in America, advocating and teaching "queer theory" to undergraduates, who ate it up.

Yet something very odd and unexpected happened in Butterfield's life. After she wrote an article attacking Promise Keepers, an area pastor named Ken Smith wrote her back, encouraging her to think through her worldview. It was a gracious letter, but Butterfield threw it away.

It didn't stay in the trash for long, though. Butterfield dug it out and wrote back to Smith. The pastor invited her to church (pastors do this!). They began to converse about a wide range of issues, including the Bible, saving faith, and homosexuality. Butterfield found herself inexplicably drawn to this old-school Presbyterian congregation, shocking as that was to her.

One day, Rosaria went to church. She was scared, self-conscious, and out of place. But she went. She kept going. And over time, something glorious happened: She was converted. She later reflected on the event for *Christianity Today*:

The church that had been praying for me for years was there. Jesus triumphed. And I was a broken mess. Conversion was a train wreck. I did not want to lose everything that I loved. But the voice of God sang a sanguine love song in the rubble of my world. I weakly believed that if Jesus could conquer death, he could make right my world. I drank, tentatively at first, then passionately, of the solace of the Holy Spirit. I rested in private peace, then community, and today in the shelter of a covenant family, where one calls me "wife" and many call me "mother."[3]

All this happened because a Christian reached out to a fellow sinner. When Rosaria came into the church fellowship, she didn't see a perfect group of humans. She saw real, flesh-and-blood people. There was something happening in this church, something life-giving and great. By the power of the Spirit, people in the congregation were finding joy and happiness and endurance. God was lifted up; God was working in the lives of his people.

So it may be for you, and me, and the churches that God gives us the privilege to join and serve and enjoy.

8 RISKY EVANGELISM: BUILDING AN EVANGELISTIC WITNESS

Afraid?' murmured the Rat, his eyes shining with
unutterable love. 'Afraid! Of Him? O, never, never!
And yet—and yet—O, Mole, I am afraid!"
    —KENNETH GRAHAME, *The Wind in the Willows*

I WANT TO TELL YOU A STORY ABOUT A GIRL FROM ancient times.

She was a young woman possessing a quiet spirit. You might have found her type in any age—sweet, kind, and modest. If she were around today, she might be a fixture at youth group, a fan of Hillsong Music, and a devotee of a local coffee shop. Whatever her musical interests, you would know you could count on her, because behind her quiet and selfless demeanor was a strong faith.

Her name was Blandina. She in fact never sang a Christian rock anthem or visited a cafe, because she lived in the second century in present-day France. Hers was a humble life. In reality, it was a hard life. She was a slave girl.

With many others in Lyon, Blandina had become a Christian

around AD 177. An elderly pastor named Pothinus had labored for years to spread the gospel in the area, and he had seen much success. People from all levels of society came to faith, including slaves like Blandina, from a place called Lyon in France.

Lyon was the main city of Gaul, which was part of the Roman Empire, still the world superpower at the time and officially pagan in nature. Seeking unity, the emperor Domitian had made Christianity illegal during his reign from AD 81 to 96. This did little to stop the spread of the faith, however, and actually seemed to intensify it. Blandina was one tiny part of this unquenchable trend, anonymous and unnoticed.

Until, that is, the persecution in Gaul reached fever pitch.

The anti-Christian spirit in Lyon grew so great that household servants suspected of being Christian made up outrageous accusations against believers to save their own skins. Charges such as incest and murder were thrown around. In the ensuing fracas, Blandina and many other Christians were taken into official custody. The odds of their survival were not good.

In short order, Blandina's life was upended. With others, she was tortured under interrogation. Such official action was not fact-finding in nature; it was designed to break the will of the Christians in order to justify their impending deaths. Blandina was not a strong girl. She was not hearty. Her torturers were trained soldiers of tough fiber. On the list of tasks for a Roman warrior, subduing young girls was easy. Ratchet up the pain, break some bones, and get the job done.

That should have been what happened to Blandina. However, she did not die on the rack. Though she was tortured "from morning till evening" until her body was mangled, no amount of pain led her to confess error in being a Christian. She seemed to gain strength, in fact, when in the midst of her torture she cried out, "I am a Christian, and there is nothing vile done by us."[1]

This was a woman, a believer, of whom this world was not worthy.

CAN WE FIND THIS KIND OF STRENGTH TODAY?

Whew. I feel like I need a walk around the block after an account like that. That is the kind of real-life story that will, if you're not careful, grab ahold of you and never let go.

This, I would propose, is exactly what many of us need today. We've established thus far that many of us could use some encouragement. Because of cultural pressure and other factors, many of us are tempted to live in a way that avoids sacrifice rather than embraces it when it is necessary to honor Christ.

We see cultural pressure and the costly nature of Christian faith in a secularizing culture, and we recoil. *Is this* really *what God requires of us—to be unpopular and unsuccessful and even* hated? *That's not what I got into this for. I was promised prosperity and favor and blessing. I was told that in coming to Jesus, the whole world would lie down at my feet. Raises would happen, friends would be made, difficulties would cease, sickness would end, and on the list goes. Now I'm making my way through life, and none of that is happening, and I'm seriously considering* getting out.

This is an entirely natural way to think today. The challenges we discussed in chapter 1 are real, painfully real. But here's the thing: God has something better for us. As we talked about in chapter 2, he offers a gospel to believe and a kingdom to serve. He doesn't want us to hunker down; he wants us to put it all on the line, risk everything, and experience the joy that comes from losing yourself in the only cause that counts. That's the faith that comes from Christ; that's the message we learn from the parable of the talents (Matt. 25:14–30).

That's what the life of Blandina, and countless martyrs alongside her, teaches us.

BUT DO WE *REALLY* HAVE TO SUFFER?

But does this really have to mean suffering? Can't we be faithful like Blandina and yet also be liked?

These are questions that some professing believers are asking today. Sure, Blandina and others gave their lives for the gospel. That is heroic, they say, and we appreciate it. But could we possibly find a less stubborn way to live, one that lets us be Christians and *also* allows us to be friendly with a secular world? Does the Christian witness, the public sharing and embodying of the gospel of Jesus Christ, really require *this* kind of sacrifice?

Some younger evangelicals want to be Christian without the sting. Rachel Held Evans, a gifted writer, voiced the mind of many when she wrote, following the passing of a marriage amendment in North Carolina, "My generation is tired of the culture wars. We are tired of fighting, tired of vain efforts to advance the Kingdom through politics and power, tired of drawing lines in the sand, tired of being known for what we are against, not what we are for."

She continued: "*Young Christians are ready for peace. We are ready to lay down our arms. We are ready to stop waging war and start washing feet.* And if we cannot find that sort of peace within the Church, I fear we will look for it elsewhere."[2]

Jonathan Merritt, a young Baptist writer, has voiced similar desires. In an editorial for *USA Today*, Merritt suggested that "a distinctive way of being Christian in the public square—a softer, less partisan way—is emerging. And this cultural change could be the very thing our faith needs to survive."

He continued by noting how many young evangelicals want to be seen as sensitive bridge-builders:

> Christians are awakening to the ways in which our cultural coarseness has affected their own community. They've heard their leaders resort to extreme rhetoric, insults and name-calling, whereby those who disagree with Christians are accused of being unpatriotic, pagans, baby-killers and anti-God. They recognize that this trend has led to 70% of non-Christians ages 16 to 29 saying Christians are "insensitive to others," according to the Barna Institute . . . Today's Christians are not seeking ways to "divide and conquer" but to "partner and achieve."[3]

It is not wrong, of course, to seek common ground with unbelievers wherever we can. It is a *bad* idea, furthermore, to seek to be hated as much as possible. Being hated, of course, doesn't mean our faith and trajectory are on point. Sometimes, we Christians are so eager to reject the world that we seem to go out of our way to be disliked.

We shouldn't commend that, and I don't.

IS THERE SOMETHING MISSING, THOUGH?

But there is something missing in these kinds of analyses, something—I don't know—Blandina-like. I smell a lot of earth in these plaintive essays; I don't smell much of heaven. There's considerable energy proposed here for the purpose of Christian acceptability. "Let's re-brand," some are saying. "Let's get popular. Let's leave aside the divisive stuff, the heavy truth claims and the unpopular social stances, and let's be liked for a change."

Friends are nice, and civility should be a goal of ours. But . . . what about the early church? What about the price it paid for its faith? Was Blandina's death in vain? Should she and her fellow martyrs have played things closer to the vest? If Blandina had adopted, say, a less direct and bold witness, might she have lived? Would people have been less upset with these rabble-raising Christians?

Was Blandina unwise, in other words, by being so bold and world-defying? Maybe her witness should have been "softer."

Public expression of Christian faith won't *always* result in being murdered, to be sure. But if we think that the faith doesn't require risk, and will not invite personal sacrifice and even cultural shame, I think we've missed something huge in Scripture.

Blandina wasn't unwise. She was living a gospel-driven, risk-taking life. This is what fearless, God-centered faith will look like in a hostile culture. In seeking to "make more" talents— glorifying God through righteous witness that stores up crowns and treasures in heaven (Matt. 6:20–21)—we will almost certainly face opposition.

Perhaps even to death.

This is utterly the opposite of the way we are tempted to

think today. The comments of Evans and Merritt show us what we already feel: that many Christians, and especially young Christians, want to fit in. We want to be liked. We don't want to be hated. We want to represent our faith in public, sure, but we have little stomach for doing so on issues and causes that divide people. That's really the heart of it: we don't want to be dividers today. We think about past Christians, perhaps leaders from the 1980s or other eras who exhibited a "take no prisoners" approach in their evangelical witness, and we rightly see that we need to speak with as much charity as we can.

But we're tempted beyond even this necessary realization to fear the culture's wrath. We don't want to be ostracized today; at just about any cost, we want to be accepted.

The problem with this thinking is simple: we're often attacked when we're doing exactly what we should in the name of Christ (Matt. 5:10–11). The wicked principalities and powers of this world (Eph. 6:12 KJV) love it when Christians, after boldly sharing the gospel and standing for biblical truth, think to themselves, *Man, I bungled that.* They exult when a believer gets a hostile response to his or her witness and then thinks, *I really messed that up. What a miserable evangelist I am. I am NEVER doing that again.* The principalities and powers of evil squeal with pleasure when, in the middle of sharing the gospel or speaking up for biblical principles, we start to detect some coldness in the crowd and feel our faces getting red. We cut off our witness with a hurried "But that's just my belief—I'm not saying everyone has to bow to what I believe."

That gets the other side—the forces of evil that oppose us—cheering, I assure you.

Jesus, to the contrary, loves it when his people fight past

embarrassment, risk social standing, and ignore nasty looks to lovingly share the gospel (Matt. 5:10–11). The angels applaud when a fearful Christian takes a risk and transitions the conversation to telling a friend who wants to be affirmed in her sin that such behavior will lead to judgment, and that God has offered sinners infinitely better life and hope in the death and resurrection of his Son.

God is glorified when his children embrace a life of bold faith and structure their whole lives around gospel witness, whether this means moving to a foreign country, using your lunch break to engage with unsaved coworkers, or working in an after-school program to make meaningful connections with needy children.

So, if the equations are

Winsome and bold gospel proclamation = hatred

or

Softer and more popular witness = acceptance

then, my friends, choose the first, over and over again.

TODAY, CONSIDER YOURSELF THE MOST BLESSED PERSON ON THE FACE OF THE EARTH

It is an unusual thing to be able to speak words that will echo down through the ages. Few of us have public opportunities to do so.

I distinctly recall a video of Lou Gehrig, the great first baseman of the Yankees from the 1920s and '30s, speaking in his final appearance at Yankees Stadium. "Today," he said, his voice echoing around the stadium, "I consider myself the luckiest man on the face of the earth."[4] Gehrig was dying. Thousands of people wept with him as he spoke these words and captured the sense of connection between a beloved athlete and his fans. It was a moment the power of which not even a born-and-bred Red Sox fan can deny—and it showed the incredible forces of public communication.

I remember being similarly moved by a man who spoke in the same era for a far more important cause. King George was a lifelong stutterer, and he dreaded public speaking. Yet the duties of the English crown required that he lead the nation through speech. As the Academy Award-winning movie *The King's Speech* makes painfully clear, the king's early efforts along these lines were disastrous. One picks up that same microphonic echo as in the Gehrig video, but the king has no memorable line that follows his first few words. He starts, and then stops. He's the monarch of England, for crying out loud, but you want to put your arm around the guy and cheer him up. He later learned to speak effectively to great crowds, and showed courage in getting to that point.[5]

Evangelistic witness on the part of Christians calls for a similar kind of courage.

If we are going to tell the world that Jesus died to save sinners, and that eternal life is found in him and him alone, then we will have to put it all on the line. We may not have to do so in so public a setting as have past witnesses, but all of us will be required to stand up and be counted, to speak up and be hated.

I've had my own such occasions. I'm not some worldwide evangelist. But over the years, I've had many opportunities to talk with friends about the Lord and his gospel. Some of these conversations went great; a few of my friends professed faith in the risen Christ. Some of them were just so-so; we had a nice chat, shared our views, and went our separate ways (with me praying that my friends would embrace the cross).

But some of these evangelistic opportunities, in college and after it, were rough. There were a few occasions when the person with whom I spoke grew angry or defensive. Sometimes I built a friendship with a person, tentatively shared the gospel, and then saw him or her back away from me. In some cases I said things in a way I would likely edit now; we are all works in progress when it comes to boldness and our gospel presentation.

Whatever response we draw, we've got to know this: evangelism is not easy. It's not supposed to be. It's challenging to tell someone that he or she is lost, in danger of coming judgment, and in need of wholehearted repentance. That's not a light and airy message. It's a world-changing message, one that calls our entire lives into question. It's a loving message, but love in a biblical sense is not mushy or weak. Biblical love is transformative, powerful, renewing, redeeming, cleansing.

As human beings, in our sin, we don't naturally want that which we need most: love. So the duty that should be most peaceful and joy-filled—announcing the kindness of God—can become a difficult task. I've seen this; I'm guessing you have as well, or will.

Just remember: evangelism is an act of courage. It stems not from anger, or condemnation, or hatred. It springs from love, love for those broken by sin like us, lost and without any hope in the world.

If by the grace of God we will reach the needy and restore the fallen, we must be courageous.

HOW TO GET THERE (BOLDNESS)
FROM HERE (NOT BOLDNESS)

So maybe you're with me so far. You're fired up by Blandina's stunning example. You see that you're tempted to play down your faith, to hide your light under a basket, as Jesus memorably put it (Matt. 5:15). You might even see that you love Christ but don't really *want* to be bold. You're not some super-apostle; you understand that if an odd opportunity presents itself to "be persecuted for righteousness' sake" (5:10) that's cool, but you're just a normal Christian who wants to keep on keeping on.

Let me encourage you to approach your Christian witness with a few things in mind.

Remember that all of life is witness. As I mentioned earlier, we too often think of gospel "witness" or "mission" as something we do at a certain time in the week. At other times in our regular lives, we're *not* doing it. We need to rethink this. All of our lives should be witness. In reality, this is not a new idea, but an ancient one.

The ancient Israelites were to be a continual light to their children, for example. They were charged by Yahweh to teach their offspring that "the LORD is one" (Deut. 6:4). This was supposed to be communicated at all times, as we saw earlier in Deuteronomy 6:6–9. This is true for us too. We should teach the truth about God and communicate the gospel of Christ to our children in specific times. But the witness of the Israelites went beyond this, and so should ours.

We'll teach our families minute by minute, and we can proclaim and show that Christ has saved us at work, talking to parents at the park, on the bus, at intermission at a concert, at the local Starbucks, and everywhere in between. We can *both* preach the gospel in a way that makes sense to the context and live according to the gospel. We can, for example, show the fruit of the Spirit at all times. That will be an obvious witness to those around us.

So, talk to the mailman as a witness; go to your spinning class as a witness; use Facebook as a witness; sell socks on Etsy as a witness; answer the door as a witness; pin things on Pinterest as a witness; raise your children as a witness; drive in busy traffic as a witness; do laundry as a witness; create playlists on Spotify as a witness. Be bold and unapologetic. You do not need to be sent by an agency to be a fearless agent of the gospel. Your local church is training you for this role, week after week. The Holy Spirit is inside you. This is the commissioning you need. Gospel work isn't for a half-hour slot every other week.

Your whole life is witness.

Living in this way is not confining. It's liberating. It will fill moments that previously felt wasted with purpose. Ministry isn't for the super-Christians. Every believer is a member of the "kingdom of priests" (Ex. 19:6; Rev. 1:6). All of us offer service to God. We can all risk everything for him. We can live every day for him.

Remember the incredible importance of witness. You will be a bolder Christian in your corner of things if you regularly call to mind just how important such work is.

Sometimes we act as if God is going to do it all. But in reality, God has called us to carry out the mission with him. This is part of the remarkable story of the New Testament. Jesus began the work of the kingdom when he came to earth. The majestic rule of God became visible and tangible as Jesus, the Messiah, performed miracles and taught as only God can teach. Though his disciples struggled to understand him, Christ's true identity emerged as time passed by. Jesus undertook a new kind of kingship, however. He ascended not a throne but a cross. On the cross he canceled the debt of a wicked people and overcame the powers of darkness.

We may assume that things stopped there, and we're all left to marvel at what Jesus accomplished. From there on out, God would lead people to see this wondrous truth, and salvation would be like a zap from the sky.

But that's the thing: while God does all the saving of sinners, he calls his church to take up the work of the gospel. This is what the book of Acts shows: the first Christians began to spread the news of eternal life in Jesus' name to everyone they could. Their story is intended to give way to our story. We are called to join them in promoting the gospel in all the world.

Is everybody supposed to be a Paul? An Apollos? A Stephen? Trotting the globe, leading the mission? No. Many of us are called to labor right where we are. But this must not obscure the fact that as believers, every last one of us is called to be a witness. The instruction Christ gave to his apostles is for us as well: "But you will receive power when the Holy Spirit has come upon you, and you will be my witnesses in Jerusalem and in all Judea and Samaria, and to the end of the earth" (Acts 1:8). The Holy Spirit did come upon the disciples of Christ, empowering them for faithful gospel proclamation (Acts 2:1–4). He does the same for every Christian today. The "sealing of the Spirit" is an empowerment for witness, as we talked about in chapter 3. A lot of times we focus on the Spirit's work in other areas, but we must fix this in our minds: *God has given us the precious Holy Spirit to light a fire in our hearts, and to enable us to carry that fire into the world so that fellow sinners may be rescued from eternal condemnation.*

So we're not supposed to gaze up at heaven, waiting on spiritual rain. It is essential that you and I recognize that God has given us a very important role: we are to be witnesses of Christ. We don't have a choice in this matter. Every Christian shares this call, though we will naturally play different roles in the movement. Not all of us have the gift of evangelism, but all of us have the charge to evangelize.

This will likely feel daunting to many of us. But we can trust in the empowerment of God to lead us. We don't lack anything that we need for this mission. We know the gospel, and we possess the Holy Spirit. Start here; go anywhere. There's not some evangelistic secret you must unlock before you can witness effectively to people. It's important to listen and learn what you can about others. But the gospel is "the power of God unto salvation" (Rom. 1:16).

Pray for boldness, and act in boldness. If you fail, try again. I've seen God give me the words I needed in many situations in which I felt awkward and afraid. I still do, and I would guess that I always will, at least some of the time. My cheeks get hot, my mouth gets dry, and I don't know what exactly to say.

But then God gives me the courage to speak. He's so faithful, and so kind.

He will do the same for you.

Remember the incredible power of a simple witness. Let me give you a few examples that play this out.

One of my friends was surfing channels one cold Maine night and happened upon the *700 Club*. He didn't know the truth about his sin and his need for a savior. He wasn't expecting to make a life-changing decision while he was passing the time. He was doing what millions of us do: turn on the TV, zone out, and wait for sleep to take over. Something clicked, though, as the gospel was shared. He's since become a strong believer, a godly member of his local church, and is raising his kids to know the Lord.

Another friend of mine was walking on the campus of the University of Maryland. He had seen "street preachers" before but paid them little mind. He was in business school and had little time for demagogues denouncing passersby. But something changed one day. He realized that in his quest to get everything, all he could in business, he was chasing the wind and would end up with nothing. The preacher's words about Jesus' death and resurrection pierced him. He was saved on the spot. Since then, he's gone on to be a ministry leader with a thriving family.

I think also of a former atheist named John Joseph, whom I heard speak at the Together for the Gospel conference before 8,000 attendees. Just a few years ago, he was trapped in lust. Beyond that, he was a cocaine dealer. This guy was the type you see and think, *Wow. That one's beyond my powers. Not sure anyone's going to reach him.* But God is in the business of blowing us away. This young dude, looking like a Hollywood movie star, went to his local Blockbuster one night. He picked up Bill Maher's *Religulous*, an open attack on and mockery of religious belief. This guy usually liked Maher's stuff, but in this film he pushed too far and—even in the eyes of a fellow atheist—didn't seem fair to Christians.

So, John got online, googled "Christianity Atheism debate," and ended up watching videos of a spellbinding apologist named Ravi Zacharias. It was like Saul on the Damascus Road. John was struck dumb. He next came across Desiring God Ministries, which features the teaching of Pastor John Piper, and listened to sermon after sermon. In the course of this he was converted to Christ and transformed. He's now a member of a strong church in Washington, D.C.

We could go on and on, my friends. What do we see in these and other testimonies? That God is great and merciful to sinners! That awesome truth aside, we see also that our witness is important. The work we do matters. Our preaching of the gospel is not dumb. We will feel that way; Satan will discourage in the moments when we do break free of fear and awkwardness. He'll ambush us emotionally and cause us to doubt that we've said the right words. He'll paralyze us by making us think that no good could ever come from *our* witness. If only God had sent someone else, someone who actually knows what he's talking about.

These are lies from the pit of hell. But they will come. This is a natural part of a bold witness. Expect, as Jesus said, persecution. Plan for opposition. Ready your heart for it.

Keep pushing. Keep trying. Keep praying.

Your witness is important. You don't need to be a super-Christian. You don't need to be a missionary (though that is sensationally important work). You need to recognize the task God has given you, and invest where you are. It may not always be the case that you can share the whole gospel, either. Perhaps you take time in a certain situation to build trust and establish a friendship. Don't condemn yourself in that case. When it is right to speak up, you'll know. Sometimes we need to be direct, and sometimes we need to allow people to observe how we live and see how God works to redeem sinners.

There isn't one way to evangelize. Provided we work to share the gospel, we can use wisdom and discretion to fit our witness to the context. That's not a bad thing that should cause us to feel shame; it's a good thing.

Be a bold evangelist through your church and your work. We've already talked in chapter 7 about how to plug into your church; as you do so, you'll find yourself naturally having opportunities to share the gospel. That's terrific.

Through youth outreach events, parenting classes, involvement in your church's mercy ministries, teaching English as a second language, and much more, you can partner with fellow members to strengthen your own witness and your church's evangelism. If you're not naturally bold as an evangelist, if you've never really reached out to anyone to share the good news of Christ, then the church should be there to help you. We don't want church programs for their own sake, but if they're genuinely enabling evangelism to happen, they're great to join.

You don't need to be the person sharing the gospel up front, but even just being a part of outreach events is a deeply meaningful way for you to help your local church fulfill the Great Commission.

I was part of a great church that started an "Exploring Christianity" program for unbelievers who wanted to learn more about the faith. They invited area folks for a meal at the church building, followed by a brief, accessible talk on an aspect of Christianity. It was a remarkably fruitful undertaking, and it allowed church members of all types to be involved in evangelism. It was a "conversation-friendly" zone, which helped people who might otherwise feel awkward talking about their beliefs open up (on both sides).

Plus, they served—I kid you not—the tastiest brisket I've ever encountered. My mouth is watering as I write this.

My hunger aside, this is the kind of program that churches should have and that members should join. You don't need to be a lone-wolf evangelist to please the Lord. We sometimes think if we're going to be faithful to Christ, we each need to be a spiritual Jason Bourne, singlehandedly saving the world from spiritual disaster. That's not true.

Support global gospel work. Every Christian should ask the question, given that the Great Commission is given to the church as a calling, as a matter of obedience, *should I leave my home to take the gospel to people who have never heard it and cannot hear it because, well, it's not there?*

All of us. Is that where God would have us go?

Don't assume he isn't calling you, or won't call you, just because you're not presently desiring such work. It may be that a door opens for you to undertake this momentous charge. If so, awesome!

But not all of us can or will go. Many of us won't. Does that mean our involvement in global missions, in the fulfillment of the Great Commission, is therefore minimal? We scan the bulletin insert about missionaries in church on Sunday, and that's it? Not at all.

As David Platt has shown in his books *Radical* and *Radical Together*,[6] every church, big, medium, or small, should be giving its members a sense for global gospel work. This isn't only a cause for some super-passionate congregations. It's the work that God has called every church, and every believer, to engage in. A major way this takes shape in the life of an assembly is for the church itself to be collectively giving a good amount to missions.

How does this happen? By individual believers and families giving sacrificially and generously to support the work.

Think of Paul's words to the Philippians:

> It was kind of you to share my trouble. And you Philippians yourselves know that in the beginning of the gospel, when I left Macedonia, no church entered into partnership with me in giving and receiving, except you only. Even in Thessalonica you sent me help for my needs once and again. Not that I seek the gift, but I seek the fruit that increases to your credit. I have received full payment, and more. I am well supplied, having received from Epaphroditus the gifts you sent, a fragrant offering, a sacrifice acceptable and pleasing to God. And my God will supply every need of yours according to his riches in glory in Christ Jesus. To our God and Father be glory forever and ever. Amen. (Phil. 4:14–20)

The Philippians did what every church—spurred on by its members—should be doing: giving generously to the work of worldwide gospel promotion. We can do so without fear or worry that we're taking undue risks in giving to missions. Yes, we risk financial security and material comfort (to the extent anyone can actually possess it). But what do we gain? We gain joy. We are able to know that God is pleased with our sacrifice.

And we can know that he will not abandon us, but will generously give all that we could ever ask or need in Christ (2 Cor. 9:8).

That, and not guilt, is our motivating impulse for all our sacrificial living, including our giving.

There's much more that we can do to support gospel missions: serve on committees dedicated to it, host missionaries when they're on furlough, train our children to have a heart for unreached people all over the world, go on mission trips to serve missionaries in the field (it's ideal to take kids along so they can see the work of the gospel), or use our business abilities (or other abilities) to help start viable commercial enterprises in places hostile to the gospel. The business-as-mission movement has really picked up steam in recent years, with groups like Access Partners (http://www.access1040.com/) and others leading the charge.

The key in all this is to find, through prayer and counsel and biblically informed self-awareness, what you like to do and are ready to do in order to push the gospel into your community, your country, and your world.

CONCLUSION

Blandina's inquisition, covered in the introduction, gave way to the gladiatorial games. Now, as if her previous tortures weren't enough, Blandina faced death by public spectacle. Surely she would give way. The end would quickly come. But the opposite was true. Left to suffer in the arena with a fifteen-year-old boy named Ponticus, the young Christian woman encouraged her brother in the faith. Unable to withstand the attacks, Ponticus died.

Reading her story, one gets the sense that time slowed down for Blandina as her body began to fail. She was scourged with cords. She was suspended on a stake in order to be mauled by animals. But her demeanor was hopeful. She did not wail; she did not beg for her life; she did not give in.

Blandina's life finally ended when a bull, crazed by the crowd and thirsty for blood, charged her. She was enclosed in a net, and she could no longer hold out. The young woman who had no voice left a witness that transcended her short life. We know the names of none of her assailants; we know hers. Never, it was said, had "a woman endured so many and such terrible tortures."[7]

You and I may never experience this kind of fate. What we do know, though, is that examples like this one are intended by God not to condemn us, but to inspire us. God isn't mad at us if we never die a dramatic death for the faith. What God does want is the faithful witness of his people. This is what delights him.

Let's pray for loving boldness in our evangelism, then. Soon all this work will end, and we won't evangelize, but will only praise and worship the Lord. We'll walk the new heaven and the new earth with the saints from all the ages, including our sister Blandina.

Together, we'll worship the one who boldly died that we might boldly speak.

9 RISKY CITIZENSHIP:
BUILDING A PUBLIC WITNESS

If you live gladly to make others glad in God, your life will be hard, your risks will be high, and your joy will be full.

—JOHN PIPER, *Don't Waste Your Life Study Guide*

ONE DAY, YOU'RE LIVING A QUIET LIFE IN AMERICA, taking walks past manicured lawns.

The next, you're in a children's institutional home in Russia.

You're used to all the comforts and conveniences of a relatively wealthy country: designer coffee, air-conditioning, trendy urban eateries for foodies, jungle gyms for the kids to play on, new sneakers, more TV channels than you can count. But now you're in an orphanage with faded green walls. The stairs threaten to give way as you walk on them. Sheetrock has fallen haphazardly along the floors. You pass a child in a hallway, strapped to a machine—apparently a standing device. The child doesn't make eye contact. He makes no sound of any kind.

That's true of the building as a whole. It's eerie. There are a hundred children in this orphanage, and none of them seems to make any sound.

Your nerves are standing on end. But you take a deep breath. You're here. You've flown for hours to be here. You've come from America for one purpose: to adopt little Kirill. He's four years old. You can't wait to meet him. Even now, steps from seeing him in person for the first time, you imagine meeting him. He'll be distant at first, but he'll quickly warm up. He'll laugh as you and your spouse play games with him. He'll run around the room in happiness. He's a boy, and boys are bound to be rambunctious.

But that's not what happens at all.

When Kirill enters the room, he's wearing girl's clothes. He smells of urine and infection. His diaper is soaked. His hands are blistered from constant sucking. His face is dotted with green slime. His eyes show no life; there is no childish flicker on seeing a smiling face. He doesn't play with the toys you've brought. He seems to be living in a kind of early death. There's no squealing, or even crying; he utters a low moan, a soft grunt.

When food is placed in front of little Kirill, he attacks it like an animal. You break up bread for him, and he seizes it, tries to eat it, but chokes on every bite. He's four, but he's never had solid food. No one has trained him to eat out of anything but a bottle.

That day ruins you. Something is now seared on your brain, something you can never erase. You have to leave for America, but you cannot stop yourself from thinking about Kirill.

This is a real-life story. Greg and Tesney Davis traveled to Russia a few years ago to adopt little Kirill. They later recounted their narrative on their family blog.[1] As you can see, it is a harrowing story.

WHAT ARE CHRISTIANS TO DO
IN A FALLEN WORLD?

Why are we covering such a moving account, though? Sure, it's great that the Davises adopted. But what's so remarkable about this?

Whatever shape human living takes, outside of Christ everyone is suffering the effects of the fall. All are in bondage (see Rom. 3:1–10). No one has ultimate hope. Some are in worse straits than others; some are in awful circumstances. Others are thriving in physical and social senses. But everyone who is not found in Christ is suffering the effects of the fall and participating in them.

This is where the Christian public witness comes in. In a thousand different ways, Christians cannot simply bide the time until we're ushered into heavenly bliss. We can't just cut the lawn and buy the groceries and play catch in the backyard. We're not able to pretend that everything is normal and nice and right, though—to be honest—our lives might actually be pleasant and happy.

If our lives are blessed in different ways, that's not wrong. Think of a text like Psalm 147, which sounds a theme found throughout the Bible, that God is often pleased to bless his children in many ways:

> *Praise the LORD, O Jerusalem!*
> *Praise your God, O Zion!*
> *For he strengthens the bars of your gates;*
> *he blesses your children within you.*
> *He makes peace in your borders;*
> *he fills you with the finest of the wheat. (vv. 12–14)*

But remember this: blessing of various kinds—happy home, needs provided for, good job—must never be an excuse to close our eyes to the plight of suffering sinners all around us. The power of the gospel is not used up when we become Christians. It's not a spiritual nitro boost that zaps us so that we're saved, then leaves us to sit on our hands, waiting for the end of time. The Lord saves us and in so doing unleashes us to be vessels of kindness and salvation in the world.

HOW JESUS INSPIRES US TO BE PUBLIC WITNESSES

Have you ever had a friend who had a galvanizing effect on people? When you were around him or her, you couldn't help but feel electricity in the air?

Many great leaders—though not all—are this type of person. I've read a good deal about leaders, like William F. Buckley. Buckley was a conservative writer and editor who pumped out more than fifty books in his lifetime. He loved to sail and often took friends on overnight trips. Here was a problem, though: he was also a syndicated columnist. This was no small column, either—On the Right, as it was called, went out to 320 newspapers across the country!

Buckley truly enjoyed sailing and was not an organized man. He would be out on his yacht, steering it with his foot (true story), suddenly remember that he had a column due immediately, and pull out his typewriter. His guests would attempt to excuse themselves, but Buckley would not let them leave. He would talk with them as he wrote, reading his sentences out loud, making jokes, but working furiously for a short burst of time until the column was finished. This was life with Buckley. It's no surprise that an entire movement formed around him. He loved ideas, people, and activity, and he constantly led others to do more than they thought possible.

He made life bigger, you could say.

This is the kind of friend we desperately need today. Many of us, as we've talked about in chapter 1 and throughout the book, are struggling for two reasons: (1) life in an already fallen world seems to be getting tougher for Christians and (2) we've been trained to think that Christianity means huddling in a corner and never risking anything for fear that we might fail. I responded directly to these problems in chapters 1 and 2.

The solution, as I've been at pains to make clear, is Jesus. He doesn't want us to fear; he wants to risk it all for the gospel and to build a big, bold life for his glory. When I read about what Jesus, the ultimate leader, said and did and accomplished, I am not able to view him as we've been trained in our day. I can't see him, in other words, as a kind of living tooth fairy. He didn't float in the air. He wasn't a gentle-voiced mystic who dulled everyone around him to sleep. He was kind, compassionate, tough, and outlandishly inspiring. I think of him as a man with a twinkle in his eye. He was restless in his soul. He had something on his mind at all times: the glory of his Father (John 5:19). He was a divine disturber of the ordinary.

He seemed to relish breaking into people's lives, doing totally unexpected things, and all so that they could know the power of life with him.

Jesus was a live wire. He was constantly leading those around him to do more than they thought they could. At the center of this leadership was his call for the church to be Christians in public, to preach the gospel of salvation through his blood and to live sold-out lives in accordance with it.

So that's what we're going to look at now. Beyond evangelism (as we talked about in the previous chapter), there are three major elements of our public witness: speaking up on behalf of our neighbor, being salt and light in tangible ways to preserve our communities, and taking sacrificial action to relieve the suffering of our fellow image-bearers.

Let's examine these three ideas now.

Love your neighbor by courageously speaking truth. There's a section in the gospel of Mark that is important to this theme. Actually, that's way understated. In Mark 12:28–30, Jesus summarized the purpose of the believer's life: "And one of the scribes came up and heard them disputing with one another, and seeing that he answered them well, asked him, 'Which commandment is the most important of all?' Jesus answered, 'The most important is, ". . . You shall love the Lord your God with all your heart and with all your soul and with all your mind and with all your strength.""'

So the Christian's entire reason for being is to love the Lord with everything we have. We laid a foundation for living up to this awesome standard in chapters 3 and 4. There's nothing more important than this.

What comes immediately after the greatest commandment is also of tremendous importance. In verse 31, Jesus details the second greatest commandment, the one that follows from the first: loving God with everything you have. Jesus tells his disciples that "the second is this: 'You shall love your neighbor as yourself.' There is no other commandment greater than these."

What do we see here? Well, several things. It's of major importance to note that loving your neighbor flows from loving God. In other words, you don't choose which of these two greatest commandments you want to follow, and then zero in on that. You're not either a "theology/truth" person or a "deeds/action" person. Sure, you may have a personal inclination; you may gravitate toward reading theology or you may not. But every Christian is called first to love God with everything they have. Secondly, we see that believers are called out of the overflow of this love to bless those around them in all kinds of ways.

Let's say it again: it's not one commandment or the other that we obey. It's both. We love God, and we love our fellow man.

We tend to think of the second greatest commandment— loving our neighbor—in very literal terms. We bake cookies for our next-door neighbors. Or we watch their dog when they leave for vacation. We wave hello to them when we're leaving for work, and we ask them how Little League baseball or work or the holiday season is going. All these deeds signify healthy forms of communal engagement. They're legitimate applications of this verse. I especially enjoy the baking of cookies, as it allows me to sequester a couple of my wife's delicious chocolate chip cookies before they exit our home.

But here's the thing: there's much more to this concept than small acts of kindness, God-honoring and evangelistically helpful as they are.

Loving your neighbor means that you seek his best. It means that you view him in biblical terms: as an image-bearer, the special creation of God, gifted with intelligence and a moral conscience and the ability to take dominion over the world. But you can't stop there. You have to factor in human sin, which has spiritually killed us. The fall of Adam and Eve in the garden marred humanity. We didn't lose our moral sense, our conscience. We didn't lose our ability to think and reason things out. We didn't lose our capacity for subduing and stewarding the earth. But all these things were disordered by the disobedience of Adam and Eve, and judgment became our deserved fate (Rom. 6:23).

So we all bear the image of God, but in our natural sinful condition, we don't naturally obey and honor him as he deserves. Beyond that fundamental failing, we are instinctively pulled away from wisdom, from what is best for us. We get our priorities wrong; we don't think rightly. We pursue morality, but not biblical morality, and not in the Christocentric way we should. We worship the creation, not the Creator, and so we make good things into idols, bestowing upon romantic partners and material goods and social causes and all kinds of things a status only God deserves (Rom. 1:24–25).

Why is this relevant to "loving our neighbor"? Because a major part of what it means to be a servant of Jesus Christ, one who obeys the two greatest commandments, is to reach out to those who live in pursuit of folly, who seek what Solomon called "vanity" in the book of Ecclesiastes, and who live according to patterns that seem liberating but are in truth enslaving. We reach out to fellow sinners personally, as we talked about in chapter 8. We build an evangelistic witness such that we're constantly seeking to lead sinners like us to see that sin has unmade them and that Christ will remake them.

But here's the part where the temperature rises for us. This duty also has a public dimension. In other words, we don't only talk to individuals in confidence about biblical truth and wisdom. We don't only love in private, in other words. We love our neighbor in *public*. There's this whole public world in which we are driven by Scripture to participate. Different terms relate to what we're calling our "public witness": the government, our nation, our culture, our society, even global issues. One of the nicest phrases that captures these realms is the "public square."

Christians throughout history have been tempted to withdraw from this public place. Some have stayed home. They've felt it best to withdraw from these difficult discussions; some have thought that even talking about matters of culture and society compromises their faith. Well, it's certainly possible that we could become too focused on politics and culture as believers. Let that be said. But I think that Scripture actually calls us to the public square. It won't let us withdraw.

Jesus summons us to love our neighbor.

Be salt and light in order to preserve and enlighten our communities. There's another powerful concept introduced by Jesus that calls us out of passivity and detachment. In the Sermon on the Mount, Jesus called his disciples to be "salt and light." He didn't mean that they should physically morph into food seasoning and particles of light. That would be difficult to pull off. He meant that his people must live and work for the betterment of humanity:

> You are the salt of the earth, but if salt has lost its taste, how shall its saltiness be restored? It is no longer good for anything except to be thrown out and trampled under people's feet.
>
> You are the light of the world. A city set on a hill cannot be hidden. Nor do people light a lamp and put it under a

basket, but on a stand, and it gives light to all in the house. In the same way, let your light shine before others, so that they may see your good works and give glory to your Father who is in heaven. (Matt. 5:13–16)

The people of God *cannot* live only for themselves. In obedience to Christ, believers must make themselves a presence for good wherever they are. Some will know far greater freedom than others. If you're living in a country that bans Christianity, you'll have far less opportunity to be publicly engaged on crucial questions than evangelicals in freer societies. But every Christian in every place can be salt and light, being a godly, courageous witness to Christ.

Salt, it seems, preserves a nation or a people; light brings people out of fear and suffering. It's remarkable to think that every Christian shares in this call. You don't need to be a political power broker to be salt and light; you aren't only qualified for this role if you're a wealthy philanthropist (though it's great for believers to play both of these roles!). Every Christian contributes. Every Christian can speak up. Every Christian should be a responsible and invested citizen of his or her country, honoring that government as much as is possible (see Rom. 13).

Jesus calls us to love our neighbor and to be salt and light. What does this mean, in practical terms? A number of things.

First, it means you will speak the truth in love on all kinds of public matters. Let's take an issue that presents itself as the modern civil rights cause: homosexuality. It's said today that if you're not for homosexuality, you're a bigot. You don't love gays and lesbians. They have been liberated to embrace their sexuality, and Christians seek to keep them in denial. We talked about this in chapter 1; it's clear that this issue is (a) extremely hot to the touch and (2) not going away anytime soon.

Believers, in other words, can't put their heads in the sand on this one. This isn't like taking a stand on candidates for the school board. That's the kind of political matter that many of us don't think much about. Homosexuality is a divisive, polarizing issue. It has picked up incredible steam in the culture. It won't only affect policy wonks in Washington, D.C. It's going to affect all of us.

I realized this when I was on Facebook a little while ago and saw pictures that a friend of mine who identifies as a lesbian had posted. She and her friends had created the float and entered it in the Fourth of July parades of a number of small towns. Seeing these photos was a poignant moment for me. It helped me see that the world had shifted. It's always been sinful. But it looks highly likely that my children will grow up in a society and culture far less influenced by the Bible than I did.

So here's the way this woman views her quest to legitimize homosexuality: it's based in freedom and hope and change. But here's what homosexuality really leads to: enslavement and despair and sin. Romans 1 and Leviticus 19, among other biblical texts, show us that homosexual practice is an abomination to God. It denies not only the truth about sex—that it is created for marriage—but the design of humanity, that men and women are complementary, different, and made for union. Because of this, homosexuality has a way of warping one's understanding of identity. There seems to be a kind of bondage that takes hold of many people ensnared in homosexual sin. In other words, their commitment to their sinful identity is such that they define themselves by it, and get lost in it.

Every person is in bondage to darkness, whether we have a natural propensity to anger, little white lies, jealousy, lust, covetousness, anxiety, or a thousand other temptations. Every sinner is equally distant from God. But some sins become our willful identity, and others do not. Few people would want to identify themselves in public as a liar or a serial killer or an adulterer. Homosexuality represents a sin that people not only practice, but tragically take as their identity.

Why are we playing all this out? Because it seems especially unloving to many homosexual people for Christians to tell them that they are trapped in sin. And this means that Christians, especially those who really want to fit in with secular culture, will feel tremendous pressure and even shame in speaking the truth about homosexuality.

But here's the thing we must remember if we are to have a bold public witness: calling sinners out of sin is not hateful. It's loving.

This is true of the gospel itself, right? It's loving for someone to have shared the good news of Christ's sacrificial death and life-giving resurrection with us. It's *unloving* for a Christian *not* to share this message of hope. In the same way, it's unloving for us not to speak the truth, whether in public or in private, about homosexuality—or adultery, lying, fear of man, pride, or lust.

It's not hateful to tell your neighbor that he or she is trapped in sin. It's kind and compassionate, and especially when you do so in a gracious and kind way. You can do it poorly if you speak without awareness of your own sin, of course. But if you're humble and empathetic, and you courageously speak the truth about sin, you are by definition being loving.

Courage and love are inextricably bound. To be courageous is to love others; to love others in a fallen world necessitates courage.

All of this relates to our public witness. We can't speak the truth about sin only in private. We have to love our neighbor. We have to preserve what we can of our moral order. We have to switch on light in a darkened place. We have to be Christians in public.

We need what you could call *winsome courage*. We're not scorching the earth with our stances, our public witness; we seek to be as kind as we can. We speak up for the glory of God, but our manner is not angry or volatile. It's winsome, as winning and loving as it can be.

This has widespread applicability. In addition to giving voice to biblical morality, this means:

- voting on matters great and small
- being a vocal citizen
- being willing to write letters to your local paper
- supporting Christian civics groups both locally and nationally that are helping lead on these issues
- attending community meetings and speaking up on crucial issues
- participating in polls, campaigns, petitions, and more
- sponsoring and encouraging Christian candidates
- supporting Christian cultural efforts in the areas of film and entertainment and television
- wherever possible, patronizing establishments and businesses that follow biblical wisdom
- involving oneself in efforts that really do promote the

common good, such as community restoration, the arts, sports programs, and much more.

Please note this: There is no shame in being a publicly minded Christian. Loving the gospel and the Savior it presents is not in *any* tension with loving our neighbor. In other words, knowing and savoring the most important truth does not mean we disregard other causes in this world. The best must not be the enemy of the good, as I've heard theologian R. Albert Mohler Jr. say many times. If you're a plugged-in Christian in the ways I've just outlined (and many others), you're not being unfaithful to the gospel. You're living out your faith in a God-honoring way. Private Christianity is not opposed to public Christianity. The church is an alien people, but we aren't beamed out of this world like the space travelers of *Star Trek* once we are converted. We are saved to be salt and light, to *be here*, and not somewhere far, far away.

What can this mean? I've personally been blessed to get involved with a pro-life counseling ministry at the local abortion clinic. I can't go every week, and I haven't seen unusual things happen most weeks when I have gone. But with fellow believers, I'm trying to be a witness unto life in a culture entranced by death.

It's a hard place to go. You're standing outside an abortion clinic; the people entering the building often tell you to back off (or worse). There are "escorts" who encourage the women going into this awful place not to listen to us, to ignore us. It's early, it's cold, and it's hostile.

It feels as though you're working on the edge of hell, truthfully.

In speaking up in this and other ministries, we're not seeking to preserve some halcyon vision of a fallen America or to beat others in the political arena. We're not engaged on crucial matters in the public square because we love the so-called culture wars. We don't. We wish everyone would embrace biblical wisdom, hence our posture of *winsome courage.*

But we also realize that if we don't speak for the unborn, then no one will. So my church is committed to the Speak for the Unborn ministry. In God's grace, we've seen several women leave the abortion clinic, the place of death, and choose life for their children.

We realize as believers that the destruction of sin means that we cannot help but speak up. This is the story of William Wilberforce. Nowadays, most everyone recognizes the evil of slavery. But it was not so in eighteenth- and nineteenth-century England. The slave trade flexed its awful muscle over the Atlantic, causing untold suffering and death for millions of Africans. Wilberforce fought for decades against the slave trade, speaking against it when no one else would. He championed an unpopular cause, and he experienced many setbacks, but ultimately, the Lord used Wilberforce not only to outlaw the slave trade but the institution of slavery in Great Britain. It is not a stretch to say that few men in history have been so powerfully used for righteous causes. The example of Wilberforce inspires us to love on behalf of fellow image-bearers, many of whom have no other champion and no other means of freedom.

So must the example of courageous Protestant leaders like Dietrich Bonhoeffer, who opposed the evil Nazi regime in World War II (profiled powerfully by Eric Metaxas in the book *Bonhoeffer*[2]), and Martin Luther King Jr., who opposed the racist social structures of America in the postwar years. There is a long and noble tradition of people holding Protestant beliefs who took biblical positions on divisive social questions in public. Many of them suffered greatly for their courage.

But they are vindicated by history, as you and I will be if we promote biblical wisdom and endure persecution for Christ's sake.

Get involved through deeds and actions. Christians must be courageous. Our courage must take the form of actual speech. We can't simply nod our heads to true statements in church. We've got to actually get into the world, enter the public square however we can, and speak love through courage.

But there has to be a second component as well: we've got to have practical skin in the game. We've got to speak up. That's nonnegotiable (Matt. 5:10–12, 16). We're *supposed* to be hated by unrighteous people for being clear about biblical truth; that's a sign, ironically, that things are going right, not wrong (according to, well, Jesus Christ).

Something is missing, though, if we talk a great game but don't take practical steps to love our neighbor and be gospel salt and light. In the same way every emperor needs clothes to go with his authority, we need deeds to go with our proclamation.

We're not only called to speak. The Bible certainly does expect us to speak up such that we may well be "persecuted for righteousness' sake" (Matt. 5:10). But it also calls us to sacrificially involve ourselves in addressing the fallenness of this world. In fact, you could say that the Lord intends for these two priorities to work together, and to show the world that the church devoted to Jesus Christ is both courageous and sacrificial (much like her namesake).

Think about texts like James 1:27, which boils "religion"

down to this: "Religion that is pure and undefiled before God, the Father, is this: to visit orphans and widows in their affliction, and to keep oneself unstained from the world." If we would claim to walk purely before God, we must be practicing "actional" faith. We can't simply say, in other words, "I'm pure because I'm saved and I have really super quiet times each morning." This is essential, because we must be "unstained" in worldly terms. But it's not the whole story.

The Lord wants our faith to have an edge, to have skin in the game, to be active in the world, to be aimed in some way at those who cannot care for themselves. Too many of us reduce our faith to church attendance and our own daily pursuit of God. These things are very important. But God intends for us to be reaching into the darkness. He wants us to love our neighbors not only by speaking, but by acting on their behalf.

He wants us not to simply identify the darkness, but to plunge into it. There is absolutely zero tension in the Bible between being a "private" and a "public" Christian. In a similar way, there is no biblical tension between loving others in word (witness, proclamation) and loving them in deed. The Lord wants both, and if we only focus on proclamation (or the reverse), we miss the mark.

This is expressly what James goes on to say.

What good is it, my brothers, if someone says he has faith but does not have works? Can that faith save him? If a brother or sister is poorly clothed and lacking in daily food, and one of you says to them, "Go in peace, be warmed and filled," without giving them the things needed for the body, what good is that? So also faith by itself, if it does not have works, is dead.

But someone will say, "You have faith and I have works." Show me your faith apart from your works, and I will show you my faith by my works. (James 2:14–18)

James does not mean that we are saved by our works, our good deeds; that would contradict the rest of Scripture (see Rom. 10:9–10 and Eph. 2:8–9, for example). He does mean, though, that if we are claiming to know Christ as Savior but have no love for our "brother or sister" who is suffering, we are in a woeful position. We may not even be Christians.

What do these strong words show us? They indicate that our faith needs to take shape. Ours is not a "prosperity-driven" faith. We didn't come to Christ because we thought we would get every worldly good our hearts could ever want. The Bible doesn't promise us that Jesus will make every hardship disappear if we follow him. In fact, as we've made clear throughout this book, trusting him as Savior could actually mean that our lives get harder. This is the element of risk we take in walking the narrow way. Our souls are secure in Christ for eternity, but the fact remains that we don't know what God will do with our earthly lives. We don't know what particular narrative will give him the most glory.

So our faith is cross-shaped. We trust, and follow, and die to ourselves.

Take practical steps to show mercy to others. What does it mean for us to put all this into practice, to be Christians who don't retreat from suffering but who engage it with the gospel so that individuals, communities, and even society might flourish?

It means we find ways to care for the needy and show mercy to the weak. There is not just one manner of answering this call.

With the gospel on our minds, and the desire to proclaim the truth about salvation, here are some steps we can take. It may mean:

- adopting a child, or supporting a couple who is adopting a child
- befriending a widow who is lonely
- mentoring boys and girls in tough communities
- providing foster care (and thinking about long-term adoption)
- restoring the physical property of a person in need
- sponsoring a child to go to a good school
- volunteering in pro-life ministries
- working in after-school programs or hosting a club at your home
- teaching a class on time management, the family, or personal growth at your local YMCA
- teaching English as a Second Language classes to immigrants
- cooking meals for needy families in your area

This is just a sample list. There are innumerable other ways to show love to your neighbors in hopes of leading them to flourishing—and ultimately, to Christ. It'd be a great idea to enlist people from your local church in these kinds of initiatives. The church's focus is the preaching of the gospel, but it is also our call to "do good to everyone" (Gal. 6:10). Our primary duty is to our fellow church members, of course; we should actually be practicing all of the above *in our churches*. But as we seek to be gospel salt and light, many of us will find that there are serious opportunities for service and witness and mercy outside of the church.

It may be tough to get started. There's limited time in the week. Practical service in a James 1:27 sense, caring for the needy, is by nature costly. I mean that it often asks us to give generously and without promise of repayment. But it is also enriching. It puts backbone in your confession. It makes your faith feel real, because in fact your faith really is taking practical shape. It feels good to give.

We weren't made to be selfish and pampered and protected. We were made to serve God and to bless others.

In a fallen world, massive cultural victories will be hard-won. Few and far between. Many of the ministries in which we invest will require a great deal of effort and will not produce guaranteed results. We would love for that to happen, and we should pray ambitious prayers to an awesome God, boldly asking him to end the scourge of death and suffering and evil in our country. We should genuinely expect that he will bless our work.

But we won't labor with false hopes in our ministries. We'll persevere. We'll get involved. We'll sacrifice.

And you know what? We'll see God do something unusual in our hearts. As we keep at it, we'll likely see him move in powerful and mysterious ways in others' hearts too.

CONCLUSION

Remember little Kirill?

When we left him, he was barely alive. He had grown since his adoptive parents, Greg and Tesney, last saw him. But he had not gained weight. He was on the path of death.

There is a tremendously happy end to this story. Kirill was

indeed adopted and brought home to the Davis family. You can see the pictures of him online. He redefines "beaming" in his family photos. He has big glasses. If you've read about his story, just looking at him will affect you. The Davises discovered that he has Down syndrome. Like so many children with this condition who are loved by a father and mother, he could not look more cheerful, more loving.

So often those the world does not want are those who most stand to lend joy to it.

The Davises loved their neighbor. Their example is inspiring to me, and I trust to you. There is not just one way to serve the Lord and to build a public witness for Christ. There are many. But all of them will involve courage and love. All of them will require that we risk something for the sake of Christ and his gospel.

And all of these ways—whether adopting abandoned children or speaking the truth about homosexuality or ministering to widows or advocating for fair laws—will honor the one whose sacrifice is not only a profound example, but the means by which we may love.

10 RISKY FAILURE:
UNDERSTANDING THE STAKES

Some wish to live within the sound of Church or Chapel
bell; I want to run a Rescue Shop within a yard of hell.

—C. T. STUDD

THERE IS A KIND OF CHRISTIAN LEADER WHO SEEMS impervious to the trouble of the world. They're the type that encourage the rest of us. They have dizzying energy and rock-solid conviction. We feel scared by what we see going on in the world; they lean into the darkness and set their faces like a rock, lending courage to the rest of us as they fearlessly proclaim the gospel.

Matt Chandler is one of those guys. He's a young dude, in his thirties, with a sweet wife and a happy family. Chandler is a tremendous preacher and public speaker, the kind who grabs you by the collar and doesn't let up until an hour's gone by and the text's been exposited.

So naturally, Chandler is free of earthly problems . . . right? Nothing can touch him?

Not at all.

Chandler, the lead pastor of a huge Texas church with more

than ten thousand members, was spending time with his family on Thanksgiving morning 2009 when he suddenly, without any previous trouble, experienced a seizure. No seizure is incidental or light. This one was pretty tough though. Chandler's six foot five, and he had to be wrestled into an ambulance. In the course of that, he bit through his tongue.

Later, doctors found out that this gospel-loving leader of thousands of Christians had advanced brain cancer.

Chandler had surgery, it went well, and now he's fully back to work, with the prayers of thousands speeding his recovery. But the cancer left its mark. Initially, Chandler had a three-year diagnosis. He would have thirty-six more months to spend with his little kids, and that would be it. Now, he has a seven- to ten-year prognosis. That's great, and he's doing well. But wow! Ten more years to live, prospectively? For one of our most gifted pastors and leaders?

A journalist covering his story summed up Chandler's experience in December 2012:

> What's fitting—or, if you like, ordained—is that Chandler has never preached that the Lord smooths the paths of his followers. In fact, he often points to counterexamples. John the Baptist was beheaded. John the Apostle was boiled in oil. Saint Peter was crucified upside down. To teach that God always heals is to misread the Bible, Chandler argues. "Follow God," he once said, well before he had any idea he would fall sick. "It could end badly."[1]

It could indeed, whether unknown or nationally profiled. Death will come to us all.

A CALL TO RISK

We started off, many pages ago, with a teenage boy perched on a big rock overlooking a whole lot of water. Yes, that trembling young man was me.

We talked about fear in chapter 1, and then we moved on to consider how God calls us, despite our natural aversion to trust him, to answer the call of the gospel wild. The Lord doesn't save us and then give us a lifelong sleeping pill so we can hide out until Christ returns. He saves us and puts us on mission.

He calls us to risk everything we have for his glory.

There's no blueprint for our lives that guarantees a certain narrative though. That's poignantly true for Chandler, as we just read, but also for us. The life of gospel risk is adventurous; it is momentous; it is inspiring.

But nobody said it would be free of challenges. In fact, we should expect that they will come. That knowledge should not kill our initiative. It should awaken it. Like Chandler, we should actually ramp up the pressure on our sin and Satan. We should redouble our efforts, through the Spirit, to give God glory. We don't know how much time we have. We know we have right now, and so we need to step out in faith and embrace a big view of our lives.

This is what the Lord wants. He wants us to step out in faith. He wants us to trust him. As we saw in the parable of the talents in Matthew 25, he is the master who has gone away and who expects his servants to work in his name and in the interests of his kingdom while he is gone. That means for us just what it meant for the servants in that story: focused, bold, prayerful planning in order to take action that will give God the glory he deserves.

The parable of the talents, remember, isn't just about money management. There's an investment strategy, I suppose, but there's a great deal more to draw from this parable.

There's a whole way of life.

So we've made the case in this book for a "risky," bold life. I've shown how we can't carry out this kind of existence by ourselves. Through the atoning death of Jesus Christ, God saves us, equips us, and empowers us on a daily, minute-by-minute basis to plunge into our little corner of the world in order to do something awesome for him. The metaphor we've used in our more focused chapters is "building." This image gives us something to get our arms around. What are we doing with, say, our families, or our careers? What does parable-of-the-talents-like "risk" look like in these and other areas? I think it pretty clearly means this: you and I take a long view of things. We see our lives as investments. We seek, over the years, to construct something enduring and God-glorifying.

Gospel risk, then, is grounded in an unshakable foundation: God. It is possible through divine grace, secured through the cross of Christ and activated in our lives by the resurrection of Christ. Sin is defeated; Satan has lost; the law is kept; we are counted righteous in the heavenly courtroom, all because of Jesus. Now we are freed and empowered by the Spirit to count the cost, forsake all the paltry pleasures of this world, and live a life of faith.

That's what gospel risk is.

Your humble author is right in the midst of this. I'm right with you. I want to be bold for Christ. I want to answer the call of the gospel wild, and risk the small and fading things that encourage me to live selfishly and with minimal faith.

So I'm trying to build into my family. I'm seeking to invest in my vocation, this line of work the Lord has given me. My church needs my investment. I want to be a bold evangelist. It's my ambition to do my little part to be salt and light in the world.

None of this happens overnight. That's the whole point. It takes time to build something big and sturdy and lasting. I'm not sixty-five, looking back at the formative years of my life. I'm living them. I see where I want to go, and hope to go. But I'm not there yet.

Faithfulness and courage are required. I can't summon these in my own strength. I see my frailty and my sin and realize that I need to constantly pray and depend on a daily basis on the Lord. He's made me—and you, and every believer—a conqueror. But he doesn't intend that I set out on my own, leaving grace behind. In fact, he regularly reminds me of the need for dependence and repentance and humility. I mess things up, I disobey, and I realize afresh just how much I need him, and just how far I have to go.

I'm living a life of empowered dependence.

But don't misunderstand me for a second. My life is not guaranteed me. I have no idea how long I've got on this earth. I don't know what the work of my hands will yield. No matter what comes, though, I have set my face like a flint. I am not turning back. I'm not defeated; sin is crucified, Satan has lost, and I really can grow in discipline and victory in Jesus.

You and I have lost the world. We've let go of control, and fear, and stress, and comfort, and ease, and our wickedness. In Christ, you see, we've risked it all.

And in Christ, because of that God-given faith, we've gained it all.

BUT WHAT ABOUT THE HARD STUFF OF LIFE?

Maybe you're smiling and nodding and paying attention. You're in. You like this model. It accords with biblical wisdom, as best you can see.

But perhaps you're thinking, *This sounds like a nice plan, but . . . um . . . what about the hard stuff of life? And not just cancer. That's huge. But what about smaller, more rudimentary difficulties?*

What happens when my discipline fails?

What happens if my efforts to invest in my children are met with stony stares?

If I try to strengthen my marriage, but my spouse doesn't reciprocate?

If I pursue marriage, but I get turned down?

If I seek to build a career, but I'm laid off?

If the people at my church are unkind to me, or there's no place for me to get involved?

If I start evangelistic conversations, only to have people at work never speak to me again?

If I try to be a public witness in my community, but it's already turned away from biblical principles?

These are real questions. They demand real answers.

The goal with all this material, after all, is not to get excited one week and spiritually collapse the next. I'm not trying to get you momentarily fired up to go and do something big. I'm not intending to momentarily stoke the passion of high school and college students, and young professionals, and older Christians, such that you get heated to a flame to TAKE A CRAZY RISK but then find yourself faltering and unchanged a short while later.

We've focused on building something grand in this book, becoming something greater than you currently are through the world-shaking power of Christ's death and resurrection. It's essential that we get that. Because you know what? I guarantee you that trials are going to come your way.

This book, in other words, is not a means of escaping struggle and suffering. I'm not saying we can become spiritual superheroes overnight, blasting through whatever obstacles the world hurls our way. We are "more than conquerors," yes (Rom. 8:37). That's a transformative reality. Sin has been crucified, and no longer has power over us (Rom. 6:6). This is just awesome stuff. It changes things for you and me—for every single Christian.

But the truth about our "conquering" nature is that we must often be conquerors in the midst of trial. Think about Hebrews 11:32–38, which shows us what victorious faith looks like in a sinful world:

> And what more shall I say? For time would fail me to tell of Gideon, Barak, Samson, Jephthah, of David and Samuel and the prophets—who through faith conquered kingdoms, enforced justice, obtained promises, stopped the mouths of lions, quenched the power of fire, escaped the edge of the sword, were made strong out of weakness, became mighty in war, put foreign armies to flight. Women received back their dead by resurrection. Some were tortured, refusing to accept release, so that they might rise again to a better life. Others suffered mocking and flogging, and even chains and imprisonment. They were stoned, they were sawn in two, they were killed with the sword. They went about in skins of sheep and goats, destitute, afflicted, mistreated—of whom the world

was not worthy—wandering about in deserts and mountains,
and in dens and caves of the earth.

This is a telling passage. The people mentioned here were conquerors, right? They did incredible things, staring down death, showing might in war, acting as forces for righteousness. This is not a chastened picture of Christianity. It shows God's people as who we are in the Spirit: empowered, emboldened warriors of Christ before whom the demons tremble.

Yet note carefully what courageous Christian living may lead to: death, torture, mocking, flogging, affliction, poverty, mistreatment, wandering without a home. Does this mean these heroes of the faith weren't really conquerors after all? No. It shows us that the victory we experience in this world will primarily be spiritual. We will dismantle sin. We will refuse, like Job, to curse God when suffering or persecuted. We will triumph over our innate doubt and lust and fear and apathy. In the power of the Spirit, we will push past physical pain and weakness and continue to bless God.

All of us, though, can be very sure that we will taste the cursed fruits of this world. Suffering will affect us all in some way. There's no way to trial-proof your life. In following Jesus with all your heart, your job may get harder. Your family may disown you. Your friends may forsake you. You may have to give up financial profit that isn't rightly yours. You will have to leave sinful relationships.

You may be martyred for your faith.

We don't know what the Lord has in store for us. He does, of course. He holds his people in his hand. He never risks. He is never caught off guard. Our lives are utterly secure in him, because he is security itself. He knows the future, and he directs it perfectly according to his will. Think of what he said to his struggling people through the prophet Isaiah:

> *Fear not, for I am with you;*
> *be not dismayed, for I am your God;*
> *I will strengthen you, I will help you,*
> *I will uphold you with my righteous right hand.*
> *Behold, all who are incensed against you*
> *shall be put to shame and confounded;*
> *those who strive against you*
> *shall be as nothing and shall perish.*
> *You shall seek those who contend with you,*
> *but you shall not find them;*
> *those who war against you*
> *shall be as nothing at all.*
> *For I, the* Lord *your God,*
> *hold your right hand;*
> *it is I who say to you, "Fear not,*
> *I am the one who helps you."* (Isa. 41:10–13)

God gave his exiled people these words when they were in Babylon, captive and defeated. Some might have heard this encouragement and thought, *But God—you're not with us. We're not upheld. Our enemies aren't perishing.* Yet it was in this awful season that the Lord reminded his covenant people that he had not forgotten them, he would deliver them, and they had no reason to fear, for he was with them. All this comfort was grounded in his strength, his grace, his sovereignty. In the middle of exile, the people of God were to derive tremendous comfort from the reality of God's powerful presence, despite what they might see or feel.

So it is with you and me. We, too, are fortified by God's words to Isaiah; we're also reminded that the Lord's power extends far past this present moment to the end of all things. Revelation 19 portrays Christ as a returning warrior-king who deals death to Satan and his minions as the Messiah returns for his people. It is "in righteousness [that] he judges and makes war," according to verse 11. God controls all of eternity. He vindicates his followers. He rights every wrong, because he is a holy God, and he will soon create a world where there is no evil or injustice.

The Lord is sovereign and good. Because of this, you and I are free to follow him, and to trade lesser things for greater, to forsake sin for righteousness. We simply seek to trust the Lord, and he will do whatever is best according to his plan (see Acts 4:28).

THOSE WHO HAVE GONE BEFORE

There are numerous examples of this kind of persevering faith. Not all of the people we can think of are famous; not all of them lived a long life. They did all honor the Lord by risking their worldly lives to gain everything in Christ, though.

Think of the missionary Jim Elliot. He went to Ecuador a bright, young, Wheaton College graduate, brimming with evangelistic zeal. We're talking about a man who could have gone on to exert tremendous missionary influence in person, both by actually doing missions and by raising awareness of the importance of this great task. God, however, had a different plan by which to use Jim to raise interest in global missions. In his infinite wisdom, he decided that it would be best to allow Jim and his fellow missionaries—Nate Saint, Ed McCully, Pete Fleming, and Roger Youderian, all young and full of vigor—to be killed by the Waorani, the very people they wanted, in love, to evangelize.[2]

This was a tragedy in human terms. Yet it was also used, in time, for the saving of many souls among the Waorani. Many missionaries in successive decades have gone to the field in part because of the courageous example of Jim and his friends. Were the martyrdoms of these godly young men a sign of failure for this missions effort? Jim risked everything for the gospel; does his death at a young age signal that things went awry? Not in the least. God has used the example of Jim and his compatriots in powerful fashion over the years to accomplish his sovereign purpose; his widow, Elisabeth Elliot, became an eloquent guide to multiple generations of godly women due to the Lord's work in her life.

We're reminded in matters like this of the following text from the book of Isaiah:

> For my thoughts are not your thoughts,
> neither are your ways my ways, declares the LORD.
> For as the heavens are higher than the earth,
> so are my ways higher than your ways
> and my thoughts than your thoughts. (Isa. 55:8–9)

There is a purpose and a plan at work in our lives and the broader narrative of the world that we simply do not know (see Acts 4 for more on this). We can't find it out. It's higher than us, but here's what fascinating: that doesn't mean that it's unconcerned with us. Though we are but specks of dust in the great Biltmore of the cosmos, we matter to God, and he fits us into his brilliant plan however he sees fit.

This is especially true for the Christian, who has the joy of consciously glorifying the Lord and obeying him wherever he takes us. In the end, "success," or return on the investment of our "talents," means being faithful to what the Lord scripts for us.

That means being faithful all the way, to the fullest extent.

Even unto death.

This was true for another young, gospel-loving man. You haven't heard his name; he's not referenced all over the world in missions stories. He was a student of mine at Boyce College in Louisville, Kentucky. Shelby-Tyler Smith was an apologetics major at Boyce. He loved sharing the gospel with lost people, crafting elaborate pranks on his roommate, and getting everything he could out of his classes. He was a godly young man.

Shelby was driving with his girlfriend after Christmas in December 2012 when he hit a rough patch on the side of the road, spun out, and crashed into a tractor-trailer. He was killed instantly. His death shook up our campus. This was the first student I've ever lost as a professor.

At Shelby's funeral, person after person shared about Shelby's unusual character and devotion to the Lord. He worked a full-time job in college as a security officer, yet he consistently wrote his papers weeks before they were due (and received all A's). When he was younger and his little sister was scared at night, Shelby would make pillow "forts" for her where she could sleep. The same sister spoke with amazement in her voice as she recounted how Shelby, in visiting her at her university, struck up a conversation out of nowhere with a blind woman outside her dorm. Within minutes, the two were conversing, and Shelby shared the gospel with her, a person many overlooked and passed by.

How painful for us at Boyce, then, that Shelby's fruitful life was over. It's not wrong to see this, and to feel great sadness in such a time. This hit me powerfully when I went through the receiving line at the memorial service. A little boy ran across my path with his aunt in tow. She talked for a moment with a member of Shelby's family, then looked at the five-year-old.

"Do you know what happened to Shelby?" she asked.

The little boy thought for a moment. "He got hurt," he said, then ran away.

Few words I've ever heard spoken hit me harder than those. In that short sentence I heard a whole worldview, a theology of pain and death that began with the disobedience of Adam and Eve and echoed into the grieving present. Sin is evil. Death is terrible. We can say many words about it, or few, but it is a reality, and it will come for us all.

Is there unfairness in this? Did God fail Shelby? No. By no means. The Lord used Shelby in unusual ways for his glory and the good of others. There's no failure in this equation. There's no distrust of God and his ways that crops up from this tragedy. God owns the cattle on a thousand hills, and he owns us (Ps. 50:10). He lets us blaze a light for a little while on earth. And then he takes us home. Everything he uses us to do is precious in his sight. His will and his ways are good and trustworthy even when—from an earthly standpoint—we don't see their immediate end.

We can rest in this: however long we live, and however much we accomplish, nothing is wasted.

DO NOT FEAR

All this material applies to you and me. In risking everything for the gospel, in planning a bold course for our lives, we are not supposed to fear what may come. Heaven is our inheritance. Beyond this, we should not feel pressure to achieve someone else's life goals. There is no set path of success for us. Even when leading a "normal" life, we should make bold plans in our corner of things; we should pray continually for God's blessing and guidance; we should live in constant awareness of the way the Lord has empowered us to work on his behalf.

We must remember that he *wants* us to exchange small, distracted, defeated lives devoted to the fruitless pursuit of pervasive safety for an assertive course of existence that delights in making more talents while our master is away.

But he will lead our course. He will show us what shape this existence is to take. It may not mean a long life. It may not mean material prosperity. It may mean being imprisoned, like Paul, for righteousness' sake. It may mean suffering in big or small ways. We have no earthly guarantees; we're not shooting for anything here, ultimately. We have our eyes set on something greater, and this perspective does not leave us useless for the work before us, but fills every moment with eternal significance, no matter how humble.

As we worship a great God, we find our daily labors infused

with purpose. If the lengthy career doesn't pan out, we can serve him in a job we never would have sought. If we end up single after thinking for years that we were destined for marriage, we don't need to feel ashamed. It's not that we weren't fit for marriage, suitably attractive, or mature. It's that God desired to chart a different course for us, and wants us to be devoted to his kingdom. If we are married, but the multiple children we wanted to have don't come, we must not assume that we're now void of purpose. Perhaps the Lord wants us to rescue children from desperate circumstances through adoption, or to serve the church in ways we couldn't previously have attempted.

If we don't end up as church leaders, and our evangelistic efforts prove fruitless in earthly terms, we can still know that our service and our witness glorify the Lord, and will surely bring heavenly rewards. If we head overseas to share the gospel with unreached people (as I hope more and more Christians will do), those that have never heard it and have no means of doing so, and the work is long and hard and seemingly fruitless, we must rest in the goodness of God and trust him to accomplish his good plan.

Whatever happens with us, we can be sure of this: everything we do for the Lord honors him. Every one of us can lead a meaningful life. We can all seek to build something great. And all of us can end up more faithful, more fruitful, more joyful in the Lord than we now are.

That is how we should understand success.

And if we're pursuing Christ wholeheartedly through a life of gospel risk, here's the awesome truth: *there really is no such thing as failure.*

BUT WHERE DOES MY STRENGTH COME FROM?

Remember as you put this into practice that you're not on your own. God is on your side. All three persons of the Godhead, in fact, are working on your behalf. As we covered in chapter 3, you've got all the horsepower for a courageous life you could ever need.

Here are three points to remember when answering the question that will inevitably come up: *From where does strength come?*

1. *Strength comes from the goodness of God.* If we are going to put in work for God, we have to know who he is and find confidence in his goodness. Think about these words from pastor and theologian Jonathan Edwards:

   God himself is the great good which they are brought to the possession and enjoyment of by redemption. He is the highest good, and the sum of all that good which Christ purchased. God is the inheritance of the saints; he is the portion of their souls. God is their wealth and treasure, their food, their life, their dwelling place, their ornament and diadem, and their everlasting honour and glory. They have none in heaven but God; he is the great good which the redeemed are received to at death, and which they are to rise to at the end of the world.[3]

   We are able to know this incredible God. We can delight in him. This is the foundation, then, of our lives and our work. We trust in this good God, we know that he is not out to zap us but to give us joy in him, and so we live confidently and trustingly for his glory. He is *not* a hard master. He is a good master, and he wants us to enjoy the lives he has given us.

2. *Strength comes from the power of Christ's cross and resurrection.* Because Jesus has died and has triumphed over the grave, you and I have access to truly world-shaking power. We may wonder how we can strike out and be like the faithful servants of the parable. We can only do so because God has saved us through Christ, who was not meek and mild—as some videos and books suggest he was—but was instead a bold and self-sacrificial deliverer of his people. Because Jesus obeyed the Father and gave his life on the cross, "our old self was crucified with him in order that the body of sin might be brought to nothing, so that we would no longer be enslaved to sin" (Rom. 6:6). Do you see this? You and I can honor the Lord through the power of the cross, because our sin—our old self—was crucified at Calvary.

So now we can live righteous lives, and in the power of the cross and the resurrection, get out into the world and give glory to God through bold and obedient piety. We could say it this way: the gospel message of Jesus' saving work offers us world-shaking power for lives of bold faith.

3. *Strength comes from the Holy Spirit who lives in you.* The Holy Spirit is not simply *out there*, but is inside all who have repented of their sin and placed their faith in Christ. So we're not called to glorify the Lord by our own effort, but through the Spirit's power. This is exactly what Paul tells us in Romans 8:10–11: "But

if Christ is in you, although the body is dead because of sin, the Spirit is life because of righteousness. If the Spirit of him who raised Jesus from the dead dwells in you, he who raised Christ Jesus from the dead will also give life to your mortal bodies through his Spirit who dwells in you." Did you pick that up? The same Spirit who raised Jesus from the dead has raised you and me from the dead. But he hasn't saved us and left to do other things on his errand list. He lives *in us* and empowers us to kill sin and embrace righteousness, which is exactly what bold faith looks like. He is, we could say, the gospel come alive in our hearts and minds.

In summary, we see the call to courage in the parable of the talents, and we remember, "The power I need to obey is not outside of me somewhere. It is here, in me, and it is *the Spirit*." The Spirit, whom we discussed earlier, never disappoints us, never stops working on our behalf, never hesitates to come to our aid in times of need. He is *always* there for us, giving us overcoming power moment by moment and day by day as we walk with Christ.

SO ... WHAT ABOUT RISK?

We come, then, to this eye-opening conclusion: *following Jesus by seeking to invest the gospel he has given us in this world is not a risk*. All the force of Trinitarian power is behind us. Serving Christ in whatever calling he gives you is the surest work you can undertake in the world, because the kingdom of God will win and the gates of hell will not overcome it (Matt. 16:18). No earthly comfort, of course, is promised us. Things may actually get *harder* for us as believers than they were before we were saved. But no one who follows God ends up poorer in the end. When we come to faith, we gain everything. We get *God*. We live for eternity with him in a garden city that is a spiritual paradise (see Rev. 21). Anything we encounter *here* is not truly a risk in the sense that we often mean it.

The challenges we face are really opportunities.

So this is what the concept of gospel risk does for you: it frees you. It positions you to see life with fresh clarity. You're released from the tyranny of small expectations. You're loosed from the chains of fearing what others think of you. In point of fact, their opinions pale in comparison to God's. You're freed from the endless cycle of brand management. It's not your reputation among fellow sinners that gives you happiness; it's being a child of God.

This truth equips you to live the kind of life that (a) Jesus commends in Matthew 5:1–11 and (b) a hateful world offers you. True Christians always have been targeted for their fidelity to Christ, and true Christians always will in different ways. We need to buckle up today. Our culture has moved from its Protestant foundation, and it will continue to move. Being a sold-out follower of Jesus will not lend popularity to your social standing. It will likely hinder it in many places.

In light of this truth, discipline yourself to be an effective soldier in God's kingdom army. If you don't, you're readying yourself for failure. Remember: there is a faithless servant in the parable of the talents. If you are saved, you won't be that servant. But you're also supposed to actively turn away from his example. You need to lean into trust and sacrifice and courage. For example, the prospect of speaking the Bible's perspective on homosexuality will make your knees weak if you're not shored up by confidence in the God who rewards bold and faithful servants.

This same God will not reward those who are ashamed of him, who close their mouths when they should speak, who spend their lives on silly, selfish things and not on the all-conquering cause of Christ.

Remember this when false gospels—we talked about these in chapter 4—tempt you. Even good things can be twisted by our fallen hearts into ultimate pursuits that we foolishly think will permanently satisfy us. *If I could just have this*, we think, *then I would really be able to trust God, because that's the gift I really need him to give me.* It's not wrong by any means to enjoy or desire God's good gifts, but we've got to always remember that nothing in this world will quench our desire for God *except God.*

There is no substitute—not earthly peace, vacations, a more fulfilling job, a spouse to love, natural children, a group of friends, a prestigious degree, a band, countercultural experiences, athletic status, physical fitness, beauty, or money. These and a hundred other realities can be changed by our hearts from gifts to gospels that falsely promise us salvation and satisfaction. In fact, we will all, in our own individual ways, face these kinds of temptations.

REMEMBER THE ONE WHO WENT BEFORE YOU

To avoid following these false promises, we must remember the example of Christ.

Jesus is the one who has faithfully walked this way before us. He is the Son of God, so he walked with full awareness of the fate that was his. His life was not a gamble. It was a gift. Jesus staked his life on the ultimate task: dying for his bride, so that he might enjoy eternity with us.

When we're thinking of inspiration for our lives, this is what we need. Christ shows us that it is good and right and incredibly God-honoring to attempt great things for God, knowing as we do that we do not know the future as he did. Christ shows us that when we give everything up for the glory of our Lord, we can never fail. Even the darkest path faithfulness calls us to walk is lit by the light of God—and leads to the city where Christ himself is the lamp of all, shining in his priestly robes, resplendent in glory.

Our sin is not all that has perished in his cross. Failure has died with it. If we are zealous for holiness, repentant when we sin, and bold to build a life for the renown of our Savior, there's no such thing as falling short. Nothing is more inspiring than that.

So, get ready. Get active. Study the Word and live the Word. Your life stretches before you.

Invest it for God's glory.

The road ahead will not be easy. It won't always be happy. Your sense of adventure will wax and wane. You may forge plans in wisdom and counsel only to see them fall flat. You may face increased persecution. Through it all, though, as you repent and exercise fresh trust, God will sustain you and empower and renew you. He will ensure that whatever you face, you will be able to count all things as loss, as the apostle Paul did. Let these words of his sink in as we fade out:

Indeed, I count everything as loss because of the surpassing worth of knowing Christ Jesus my Lord. For his sake I have suffered the loss of all things and count them as rubbish, in order that I may gain Christ and be found in him. (Phil. 3:8–9)

Soon, brothers and sisters, we'll be in glory, and we'll celebrate what the gospel accomplished for us by God's awesome grace: we risked the world, losing nothing . . .

. . . and trusted Christ, gaining everything.

ACKNOWLEDGMENTS

I AM THANKFUL TO THE LORD FOR THE OPPORTUNITY to write this book. It is my hope that it will be used for his glory because that is really what "success" means for a Christian writer.

I am indebted to my sweet wife, Bethany, who was a continual source of encouragement, wisdom, and joy during the writing process. She kept our home humming while I was writing. She is a great gift to me.

My agent, Erik Wolgemuth, deserves a big thank you. Erik is a great partner in the gospel and proficient in all he does. He sets a high bar for literary representation, as does the Wolgemuth & Associates team.

I'm thankful to Joel Miller, Kristen Parrish, and the Thomas Nelson team for their high standards and hard work. Joel believed in this project from the start; I appreciate his strong commitment to this book.

To my colleagues at Boyce College and Southern Seminary, thank you for your friendship and support. This includes, but is not limited to, Dan DeWitt, Chad Brand, Denny Burk, Jim Hamilton, Brian Payne, Greg Wills, Travis Kerns, Barry Joslin, Heath Lambert, and Scott Connell. I'm remarkably blessed to serve at an institution that believes in, and makes space for, the kind of work that produces a book like this.

To my parents, Andrew and Donna Strachan, I am grateful that you raised me to know the Lord and lead a committed life for his glory. To my parents-in-law, Bruce and Jodi Ware, I'm deeply appreciative of your encouragement and counsel. I am thankful as well for good and godly friends, including KC, JA, Rob Gregory, and Jed Coppenger.

Finally, this book is dedicated to R. Albert Mohler Jr., a man of courage and gospel ambition. I am deeply thankful to call him a friend and a mentor. In classes and conversations, Dr. Mohler taught me the kind of theological worldview outlined in this humble little book, but he also modeled it with his life. Working in his office for several years gave me a first-hand picture of what it means to go all out for God's glory (to condense: it's not boring!).

Now, as a faculty member at the institution he leads in service to Christ, I remain invigorated by his example and grateful for his investment. *Soli Deo gloria.*

NOTES

Chapter 1

1. James Kelly, *A Complete Collection of Scottish Proverbs: 1721* (n.p.: Kessinger, 2009), 270.
2. Jennifer 8. Lee, "Generation Limbo: Waiting It Out," *New York Times*, August 31, 2011, http://www.nytimes.com/2011/09/01 /fashion/recent-college-graduates-wait-for-their-real-careers-to -begin.html?pagewanted=all&_r=0.
3. Judy Wachs, "After the Affair," *New York Times*, November 23, 2012, http://www.nytimes.com/2012/11/25/fashion/modern-love -learning-to-love-again-after-the-affair.html?pagewanted=all.

Chapter 2

1. *Wikipedia*, s.v. "Gangnam Style," http://en.wikipedia.org/wiki /Gangnam_Style.
2. Scott McClellan, "Vintage21 Goes Viral," Echo Hub, September 1, 2007, http://echohub.com/posts/video/vintage21-goes-viral /. To view the videos, go to http://www.youtube.com/watch?v =DDSj8sv0uKs.
3. Bob Lotich, "The Parable of the Talents," Christian Personal Finance, *http://christianpf.com/the-parable-of-the-talents/*.

4. Frank James and Alan Artner, "Unknown Van Gogh Pops Up in Wisconsin," *Chicago Tribune*, January 9, 1991, http://articles .chicagotribune.com/1991-01-09/news/9101030200_1_work-by -vincent-van-van-goghs-auction-house.

5. John Piper, *Risk Is Right* (Wheaton, IL: Crossway, 2012).

6. "NEWSWEEK Cover: Stress Could Save Your Life (or at Least it's Better for You Than You Think)," http://java.sys-con.com/node /842906/print.

CHAPTER 3

1. You can see Christopher's performance of "Open the Eyes of My Heart" at http://www.youtube.com/watch?v=IkgbDu9iDqo. He was ten at the time of the recording.

2. Andrea Gibb, *Dear Frankie* (film), directed by Shona Auerbach (2004); distributed by Miramax Films.

3. Michelle Gonzalez, "Christopher Duffley Overcomes Blindness and Autism," Autism Key, February 2, 2012, http://www .autismkey.com/christopher-duffley-overcomes-blindness -and-autism/.

CHAPTER 4

1. "Goof on the Roof, Ronald Stach Arrested," Hicktown Press, December 30, 2007, http://www.hicktownpress.com/goof-on -the-roof-ronal-stach-arrested/.

2. Tim Challies's short book *Sexual Detox: A Guide for Guys Who Are Sick of Porn* is a good help in fighting lust (Adelphi, MD: Cruciform Press, 2010).

3. Steve Arterburn and Fred Stoeker, with Mike Yorkey, *Every Man's Battle: Winning the War on Sexual Temptation One Victory at a Time* (Colorado Springs: WaterBrook Press, 2000).

4. Walter Isaacson, *Steve Jobs* (New York: Simon & Schuster, 2011).

5. Timothy Keller, *The Prodigal God* (New York: Penguin, 2008), 53–56.

CHAPTER 5

1. Bruce Ware, *Father, Son, & Spirit: Relationship, Roles and Relevance* (Crossway, 2005).

2. Joshua Harris, *Boy Meets Girl: Say Hello to Courtship* (Colorado Springs: Multnomah, 2005), chap. 8.
3. Bruce A. Ware, *Big Truths for Young Hearts: Teaching and Learning the Greatness of God* (Wheaton, IL: Crossway, 2009); J. I. Packer, *Knowing God* (London: Hodder and Stoughton, 1973).

CHAPTER 6

1. John Piper, "The Great Work of Rain," Desiring God Foundation website, November 19, 1998, http://www.desiringgod.org /resource-library/taste-see-articles/the-great-work-of-god-rain, © 2013.
2. See http://www.hobbylobby.com/our_company/our_company. cfm; http://www.hobbylobby.com/our_company/purpose.cfm; http://www.hobbylobby.com/our_company/ministry.cfm.
3. Edith Schaeffer, *Hidden Art of Homemaking* (Carol Stream: Tyndale house, 1972).
4. *The Electronic Encyclopedia of Chicago*, s.v. "Quaker Oats Co.," http://www.encyclopedia.chicagohistory.org/pages/2821.html.
5. *Wikipedia*, s.v. "Henry Parsons Crowell," http://en.wikipedia .org/wiki/Henry_Parsons_Crowell.
6. See http://www.ecfa.org/MemberProfile.aspx?ID=7863.
7. See D. A. Carson, "Is Tithing Biblical?" http://highpointeaustin .org/pdf/2007_Sermon_Notes/Notes_2007-11-18am_Is_Tithing _Biblical.pdf.

CHAPTER 7

1. Alexis Grant, "I Fell in Love with a Megachurch," Salon.com, January 29, 2012, http://www.salon.com/2012/01/29/i_fell _in_love_with_a_megachurch/.
2. See *Wikipedia*, s.v. "To Build a Fire," http://en.wikipedia.org/wiki /To_Build_a_Fire.
3. Quoted in David French, "When Our Principles Don't Survive Contact with Pain," *National Review Online*, March 25, 2013, http://www.nationalreview.com/corner/343879 /when-our-principles-dont-survive-contact-pain-david-french.

CHAPTER 8

1. John Lane, "St. Blandina and the Martyrs of Lyons," the Aquinas Site, June 2, 2001, http://strobertbellarmine.net/saints /blandina.html.
2. Rachel Held Evans, "How to win a culture war and lose a generation," *Rachel Held Evans* (blog), n.d., http://rachelheldevans .com/blog/win-culture-war-lose-generation-amendment-one -north-carolina.
3. Jonathan Merritt, "New form of Christian civic engagement," *USA Today*, upd. May 8, 2012, http://usatoday30.usatoday.com /news/opinion/forum/story/2012-05-06/evangelical-christians -politics-religious-right-2012/54791418/1.
4. You can see this video at http://msn.foxsports.com/topics/m /video/24272368/gehrig-s-farewell.htm.
5. See http://www.kingsspeech.com/.
6. David Platt, *Radical: Taking Back Your Faith from the American Dream* (Colorado Springs: Multnomah, 2010); *Radical Together: Unleashing the People of God for the Purpose of God* (Colorado Springs: Multnomah, 2011).
7. Lane, "St. Blandina."

CHAPTER 9

1. See *Our Eyes Opened* (blog) at http://oureyesopened.blogspot.com/.
2. Eric Metaxas, *Bonhoeffer: Pastor, Martyr, Prophet, Spy* (Nashville: Thomas Nelson, 2011).

CHAPTER 10

1. Tom Bartlett, "Laughter and Brimstone: Flower Mound's Matt Chandler Updates That Old-Time Religion for a New Generation," *Texas Monthly*, December 2012, http://www.texasmonthly.com /story/laughter%C2%A0and%C2%A0brimstone.
2. http://www2.wheaton.edu/bgc/archives/GUIDES/277.htm#3.
3. Jonathan Edwards, *Works of Jonathan Edwards*, vol. 17, *Sermons and Discourses*, ed. Harry S. Stout (Yale University, 1999), 208.

ABOUT THE AUTHOR

OWEN STRACHAN IS EXECUTIVE DIRECTOR OF THE Council on Biblical Manhood & Womanhood and assistant professor of Christian theology and church history at Boyce College in Louisville, Kentucky. He also teaches for the Southern Baptist Theological Seminary. A contributing writer for the Gospel Coalition, Strachan has published six books and has authored essays for the *Atlantic, First Things*, and *Christianity Today*. Strachan completed a PhD in theological studies at Trinity Evangelical Divinity School, an MDiv in biblical and theological studies from SBTS, and an AB in history from Bowdoin College. He is married to Bethany and is the father of two children. A member of Kenwood Baptist Church, he enjoys basketball and has made a rap CD.